OLD TESTAMENT
CHALLENGE

3

DEVELOPING A **HEART** FOR GOD

LIFE-CHANGING LESSONS FROM THE WISDOM BOOKS

JOHN**ORTBERG**

WITH KEVIN & SHERRY **HARNEY**

ZONDERVAN™

GRAND RAPIDS, MICHIGAN 49530 USA

WILLOW

Willow Creek Resources

We want to hear from you. Please send your comments about this book to us in care of zreview@zondervan.com. Thank you.

ZONDERVAN™

Old Testament Challenge Volume 3: Devloping a Heart for God Teaching Guide
Copyright © 2003 by Willow Creek Association

Requests for information should be addressed to:

Zondervan
Grand Rapids, Michigan 49530

ISBN 0-310-25032-3

Interior design by Sharon VanLoozenoord

Interior composition by Tracey Moran

Printed in the United States of America

03 04 05 06 07 08 /❖ ML/ 10 9 8 7 6 5 4 3 2 1

Contents

Introduction

The Old Testament Challenge (OTC) is designed to foster spiritual formation and growth on three distinct levels (congregation-wide, small group, and individual). The first level of learning is with the full community of God's people. This teaching resource can be used in the setting of a worship service or in a large class. The primary reason these materials were developed was for use in a worship service, but there could also be some application of these materials in a larger class setting.

This teaching resource is designed to give teachers a wealth of ideas as they prepare to bring a message from God's Word. These materials have been designed to provide a large pool of information on the text and ideas for preaching. From these materials, the teacher can shape and form a message that fits the congregation he or she serves. As you will discover when you begin to dig into the teaching resources, there are far more source materials and ideas than can be incorporated in a normal sermon or teaching session. You will each need to decide what materials best fit your situation, add your own personal illustrations and teaching ideas, and then form a message that fits your congregation and personal teaching style.

These materials have intentionally been developed on two levels. First, John Ortberg wrote the initial messages and preached them at Willow Creek Community Church. John developed these messages to teach them at the New Community Believers' Services. You will find an audiotape or CD of these messages in each of the four OTC kits. You will also notice that there were a few guest preachers who took part in the OTC teaching at Willow Creek.

The materials and resources from the OTC were then adapted for a second-generation OTC church, Corinth Church in Grand Rapids, Michigan. Kevin Harney continued the process of developing and expanding the materials as he preached the messages in the Sunday morning services at Corinth Church. New illustrations, creative message ideas, Power Point presentations, Frequently Asked Question sheets (FAQs), and other study materials were added and the messages were expanded. Although John Ortberg was the primary writer/teacher at Willow Creek and Kevin Harney the primary writer/teacher at Corinth Church, a whole team of teachers, leaders, and editors have partnered together to develop and create this teaching resource.

What makes the teaching resource for the OTC so unique are the many different tools offered to the teacher in this Old Testament Challenge kit. When you open the teacher's resource, you will find the following categories of material in various combinations:

- The Heart of the Message

- The Heart of the Messenger

- Creative Message Idea

- Historical Context

- Illustration

- Interpretive Insight

- Life Application

- Narrative on Life

- Narrative on the Text

- New Testament Connection

- On the Lighter Side

- Pause for Prayer

- Pause for Reflection

- Quotable Quote

- Significant Scripture

- Word Study

It is important to note that some of the teaching resources listed above will appear in every study (for example, The Heart of the Message, The Heart of the Messenger, and Interpretive Insight). Some of the other resources might appear in one message but not in another. The sixteen various components of the OTC messages contained in this teaching guide are defined in the pages that follow. As you review what each of these teaching tools offers, you will begin to get a sense for the depth and breadth of what is offered in each of the OTC message resources.

The Heart of the Message

This is a brief description of the heartbeat or central theme of *the entire message*. Each message will begin with a short section to help the teacher gain a sense of the core idea or ideas being communicated in each OTC message.

The Heart of the Messenger

Teachers and preachers can't communicate with passion and clarity until their hearts have been touched and impacted by the truth of God's Word. This section of the teacher's resource will give some direction for how each teacher can begin to prepare to study and open his or her heart to what the Holy Spirit wants to say. One of the goals of the Old Testament Challenge is to help teachers move forward in their own journey of faith. We believe the process of self-examination, deep learning, and personal growth that will be experienced while leading the OTC can be life-changing! This section will usually include a few questions for personal reflection as the teacher prepares to bring the OTC message.

Creative Message Idea

This section of the OTC teaching resource will offer a broad variety of ideas a teacher can use to bring a biblical point home with power. This section will include video pieces developed specifically for OTC messages. It will also include a number of ideas for using props or visual aids to communicate a relevant biblical truth. Some of the creative message ideas will help the teacher move worshipers to respond or interact during the message. We can't begin to cover all the creative ideas that have been developed to bring the message of the Old Testament alive, but if you take a few moments and skim through this OTC teacher's resource, you will begin to get a sense of the kinds of creative ideas that are available for a teacher or preacher. In an effort to make these ideas user-friendly, we have listed everything that is needed to naturally incorporate each creative idea into the message. Each of these ideas has been used effectively at Willow Creek or Corinth Church, or both, but we encourage you to decide which ones will connect in your particular context.

Historical Context

Throughout the teacher's resource you will find helpful notes on the historical context of certain passages. There are a number of texts we will study in the OTC that make much more sense when we have an understanding of the culture and the world of the Old Testament. The Historical Context notes are provided to help you teach about this kind of background information. These notes are not designed to be highly academic observations but are intended to help the teacher make natural observations about culture and customs that will bring the message of the Old Testament alive.

Illustration

Jesus was a master storyteller. He used word pictures to illustrate much of what he taught. In the teacher's resource we have provided many ideas for illustrating core Old Testament ideas. Sometimes these illustrations can be read just as they are printed in this teacher's guide. At other times, you as the teacher will be given ideas or direction on developing an illustration out of your own life or ministry. You must decide whether an illustration fits in your setting. Even if a particular illustration does not fit in your context, it might spark some ideas for an illustration that does.

Interpretive Insight

A huge part of teaching the Bible is doing interpretive work. We have provided solid biblical interpretation that can function as the backbone of each OTC message. This does not mean that the teacher should avoid additional study, but it does offer a great starting point. The major texts being used in each message will have a brief, or sometimes extended, section of biblical interpretation provided in the teacher's resource guide.

Life Application

In the book of James we read these words, "Do not merely listen to the word, and so deceive yourselves. Do what it says" (James 1:22). Any study of God's Word that is going to have life-changing power must include application. In each OTC message you will find ideas for life application. Sometimes these ideas are specific. They will give detailed instruction on concrete ways a congregation can respond to God's Word. At other times these applications will be broad, intended to encourage individual reflection upon a specific area of life. In these cases, the specific application will come as the Holy Spirit speaks to the heart of each person and shows where change needs to take place.

Narrative on Life

Occasionally telling a story from everyday life is the best way to bring a biblical truth home to the listeners. In this OTC teacher's guide we have captured some great examples of life narratives that speak powerfully. These can be used as they are found in the teacher's guide, or you can retell them in your own words.

Narrative on the Text

One of the unique gifts John Ortberg has as a preacher is the ability to tell a familiar biblical story in a fresh narrative form. This retelling of the story, including some natural commentary on the text, brings familiar passages alive. These sections of John's sermons have been captured in a form that can be read by the teacher. Or, they can become a source of ideas as you tell the story in a narrative form that fits your style of communication.

New Testament Connection

There are many places where the Old Testament and New Testament intersect. Because most Christ-followers are more familiar with the New Testament, we have tried to make note of natural connection points between these two parts of the Bible. Sometimes the connection is linguistic, at other times it is thematic, and there are also times when a specific Old Testament passage is used in the New Testament. You will find helpful insights on how the Old Testament passage you are studying relates to familiar portions of the New Testament.

On the Lighter Side

Humor can be one of the greatest tools in a sermon. Jesus used irony and humor in his communication, and we can learn to use it as we teach God's Word. In these portions of the teacher's guide you will find two specific kinds of humorous insights. First, we will make note of biblical passages or insights that have a humorous aspect to them. Second, we will give you ideas for stories or jokes that might hit a main theme in the message.

Pause for Prayer

Too often a teacher waits until the end of a message to pray with God's people about what is being taught and learned. Sometimes the best time to pause for prayer is right in the middle of a message. If a point has a strong life application or potential for conviction and transformation, you might want to pause right in the midst of the message and take a few moments for prayer. The Pause for Prayer sections give suggestions for when you might want to do this and how to move naturally into prayer at these times.

Pause for Reflection

We live in a hurried world. Often, we preach and teach with the clock in mind. In our busy world, we need to be reminded that teaching God's Word should always include time for personal reflection. We need to make space for the Holy Spirit to speak to our hearts and touch our lives. The Pause for Reflection portions of the teacher's guide give the teacher ideas for possible times to pause, right in the middle of the message, and to take a moment for silence. These moments can be used to listen to God, process the lessons that have been learned, and reflect on personal life application goals.

Quotable Quote

God has spoken powerfully through many of his people through history. We have collected some great quotes from Christians throughout the ages and included them in the studies.

Significant Scripture

Every sermon in the OTC teacher's guide is rooted in Scripture. At the beginning of each section of each message is a list of significant Scriptures for that portion of the sermon. Most of the Scriptures listed are included in the message notes, but some are not. Occasionally we will list a related passage because we believe it would be worth studying as you prepare your message. Most of the time there is exposition of the passages listed in the Significant Scripture part of the study, but some of the time these are simply passages we encourage you to use for reflection as you prepare your message.

Word Study

Often the background of a word in the Bible helps a passage come alive and make sense. Any time we feel a word needs explanation, we include a short background piece in a word study. Sometimes these word studies give linguistic background; at other times they simply give a broader meaning for a word that might go unnoticed if not highlighted.

David: Developing a Heart for God

2 SAMUEL 5, 6, 9, 11, 12; PSALM 51

The Heart of the
MESSAGE

This message is about the heart of God's people. God is deeply concerned about our hearts. He wants the throne of our heart to be his dwelling place. The problem is, there are many other things that are battling for the place of supremacy in our lives.

In this message we look at King David and discover that he had the same struggles we all face. He loved God with all his heart, but he faced many temptations to let other things push God off the throne. As we look at David's lifelong struggle to yield his heart fully to God, we will discover that we too can develop a heart that beats passionately for God.

The Heart of the
MESSENGER

Like David, every follower of Christ faces the lifelong challenge to keep God firmly on the throne of his or her heart. As a teacher, you will bring this message to your congregation, class, or small group. Your preparation and communication will be a journey of self-examination.

For you to communicate God's message with clarity and integrity, you will need to invite the Holy Spirit to search your own heart. Is God fully enthroned in your life? Does he rule in your heart? Are there people, habits, life patterns, fears, or anything else that have begun to take a place of supremacy in your life? Come before God with deep humility and ask him to reveal any idol, any alternative to God, that may be alive in your heart. You may want to meditate on Psalm 51 as you prepare this message.

**Brief Message
OUTLINE**

1. David's Story
2. Learning from David: Worship
3. Learning from David: Relationships
4. Learning from David: Temptation
5. Learning from David: Confession

1. David's Story

**SIGNIFICANT
SCRIPTURE**

2 Samuel 5

**NARRATIVE
ON LIFE** | The Furnace of the Desert

It is in the desert that David is really at his best. That's where his life gets shaped and defined by God. In his life, David has many victories in battle. He has accomplishments, wealth, and the praise of people. But when it is all said and done, David seems to be at his best when he is in the furnace of the desert. The dry air cracks his lips; the heat drains his energy. But in this arid place of desolate silence, David meets with God. In the desert he wrote many of the Psalms, he speaks to God, and he learns.

Rarely do God's people ask to be placed in the furnace of the desert. It would seem masochistic to ask for such an experience. Yet, God often leads his people to this place of training, discipline, refining, and preparation. Moses spent time in the desert, and so did the nation of Israel. David was trained in the desert school. Even Jesus, who never sinned, was led by the Spirit into the desert for forty days.

Sometimes God leads those he loves through a season of desert wandering. But when he does this, it is always with a purpose. When we find ourselves in the desert, we must look to God and ask, "What can I learn in this place?" We must avoid the natural reaction of running away. We must learn, as David did, that God does some of his best work in us when we are in the desert.

ILLUSTRATION | Martyrdom of Polycarp

Called upon to curse Christ, Polycarp, in the second century, spoke these words before he was martyred for his faith: "Eighty and six years have I served Him, and He has done me no wrong; how then can I blaspheme my King who saved me?"

**HISTORICAL
CONTEXT** | David's Story, Part 1

More is written about David (and by David) than any other character in the Old Testament. Hundreds and hundreds of books have been written about his life. In this Old Testament Challenge study, we will focus primarily on the years of David's kingship.

Many are familiar with the stories of David. They may have grown up seeing his life as a shepherd boy, his battle with Goliath, and his ascension to the throne played out on the two-dimensional world of a flannelgraph in Sunday school classes. Prior to 2 Samuel, David was a shepherd tending his father's flocks around Bethlehem. Samuel, the prophet of Israel, was led to the home of Jesse and was called by God to anoint David as the new king.

Soon David fights the giant, Goliath. He defeats him and becomes famous in the land. Over time, King Saul becomes incredibly jealous of David and threatens his life so much that David has to flee from Saul. He then finds himself in the desert, wandering for years, separated from his family and the kingdom. In 2 Samuel 5, David finally steps into the role of Israel's king. He conquers Jerusalem, defeats the Philistine army, and begins his kingship.

And then, at the stake in the sports arena at Smyrna, right before the end, Polycarp said: "Make me a true athlete of Jesus Christ, to suffer and to conquer; an anvil, Lord, let me be an anvil, smitten but standing firm."

2. Learning from David: Worship

NARRATIVE ON THE TEXT | **Celebrating God!**

The ark of the covenant was the closest thing Israel had to a throne for God. Over the atonement cover on the ark, the presence of God was said to dwell. It was a sacred reminder to Israel that God was with them. And David knows that the ark must be back in Jerusalem.

> **SIGNIFICANT SCRIPTURE**
> 2 Samuel 6

Thus, David gets a group together, and they go down to get the ark from the house of Abinadab. Just to give you a sense of how important this is to David, he chooses thirty thousand men to accompany him to retrieve the ark. After a long journey getting the ark back to Jerusalem, an incredible party breaks out.

We may picture Mardi Gras or the Rose Parade and think they are a big deal, but the celebration that accompanies the return of the ark is huge! The ark of the covenant is back in Jerusalem. God's presence can be felt and seen. A party erupts and rolls through Jerusalem. "David, wearing a linen ephod, danced before the LORD with all his might, while he and the entire house of Israel brought up the ark of the LORD with shouts and the sound of trumpets" (2 Samuel 6:14–15).

In this public setting, David is swept into worship. With all his might he begins to express his praise and thanks to God. This is full body, full contact, no-holds-barred worship. He is letting it loose for God.

HISTORICAL CONTEXT | **David's Story, Part 2**

The nations around Israel had kings. For many years, Israel did not. However, at their own insistence they got a king. Their first king was Saul. He had many flaws and his story ended sadly. But when David took the throne, there was a chance for a new beginning. As David's kingship began, it appeared that he would be an A+ monarch.

Israel was excited about their new ruler. Yet we must always remember as we look at the history of Israel that God had made himself available to be their one and only king. The tragedy of their story, and often ours, is that God isn't enough. They, and we, want a person on a throne to rule.

In 2 Samuel 5 we see David experience a time of great success. He has incredible success at taking back Jerusalem—this chief city of Israel. Next he defeats the Philistines, their prime enemy. As part of his victorious campaign, David decides he will bring back the ark of the covenant to Jerusalem.

**CREATIVE
VIDEO ELEMENT**

(VHS or DVD)

What's Up with That?
"The Diner" (4:50 min.).
This feature, hosted by Jarrett
Stevens, answers tough
questions from the Old
Testament in an entertaining
way. It can be used with any
session.

NARRATIVE ON THE TEXT | Not Everyone Will Understand

The king of Israel is dancing with all his might . . . in his underwear. David worships the Lord with complete abandon and disregard for what anyone else may think. This includes his wife, Michal, who is the daughter of Saul. Michal is quite disgusted and offended to see her husband, the king, dancing around the kingdom in his ephod. She is sure this will not be good for public relations. It is certainly going to make the next morning's paper. She is incredibly distressed. But David doesn't care; he is worshiping God with all his might. His attention is fixed and focused and lost in the glory of God.

ILLUSTRATION | Wild in Worship

On the CD included in your OTC kit, Jarrett tells about his wife and the wild worship sessions she has as she drives. You may want to tell a story about someone you know who is an authentic and passionate worshiper.

NARRATIVE ON LIFE | Freedom in Worship

Imagine what it may look like to be free in your worship of God. What impact would it have on you as a worshiper if you had no concern for what the person next to you sounded like or what you sounded like to them? What if you did not worry about what other people may think of you if you were truly free in worship? How would it feel to be so lost in the glory and wonder of God that you stopped thinking about what others were doing or thinking?

In 2 Samuel 6:22 David tells his wife Michal, "I will become even more undignified than this, and I will be humiliated in my own eyes." It is as if David is telling his wife, "You think this is bad? Just wait until I get going. Wait until I start worshiping God with all my might."

ON THE LIGHTER SIDE | A Linen Ephod

Right in the middle of this scene of celebration there is a side-note that can be easily missed. David is wearing a linen ephod. What is an ephod? Why is that important? Why are we given information about a linen ephod? An ephod was sort of a sleeveless undergarment that came down to about hip length. Essentially, it was really nothing more than his underwear. Of course, this has implications for how David appears and how people perceive him.

If you listen to Jarrett's message, you will notice that he has fun with this idea. He says, "In fact, to be honest with you, I'm wearing a linen ephod right now and they are incredibly comfortable. They breathe and they move so nice." You can decide if your congregation will appreciate a comment like this.

The truth is that many people have grown up in a church where worship of God was seen as a "dignified" thing. Everyone stood properly with their nice clip-on ties or neatly pressed dresses. They sang from their hymnals, knew when to stand and sit, and followed a clearly printed order of worship. It was all done in a proper manner.

This is not the picture we have of King David. He is passionate, reckless, invested, and even undignified. David's example can become God's invitation for us to enter a deeper, richer, messier kind of worship.

LIFE APPLICATION | Getting Undignified

David is lost in the glory of God, worshiping God with all his might. What would it look like if we learned to worship with all our might? How might our worship services change? What risks would we learn to take?

We may ask the Holy Spirit to fill our hearts and our churches in new and fresh ways. We may also begin taking risks as his worshipers. The key is that our outward expressions of worship be consistent with what is really happening in our hearts. Expressiveness and passion in worship are not some preplanned action that appears to be spiritual. They are a natural and free outward expression of the work that the Holy Spirit is doing inside of us. There is a consistency between our outward expression and our inward experience of God.

You may want to begin by singing praise with all your might when you are driving down the road, in the shower, or with God's people. Maybe you have wanted to lift your hands in worship for a long time, but you always resist because you fear what others may think. The next time you sense the Spirit prompting you to lift your hands, begin by simply turning them upward in your lap or right in front of you. Let your outward posture match what is happening in the depth of your heart. The key is to begin taking steps of responsiveness to God's leading in worship.

NARRATIVE ON LIFE | The Reality of Community

Our worship can be full and expressive. However, we should remember that when we worship in community with others, they are also seeking to worship. In other words, if our freedom to worship consistently keeps our brothers and sisters from worshiping, we must limit our freedom.

Oliver Wendell Holmes, a past U.S. Supreme Court judge, is quoted as saying, "Our freedom of speech ends when someone yells 'fire' in a crowded theater." Another quote attributed to him is, "Our freedom to extend our arm ends where the nose of the person standing next to us begins." In short, our freedoms, in every area of life, are limited when we are with other people. This includes worship.

NEW TESTAMENT CONNECTION

Please God, Not People

In Galatians 1:10 Paul writes, "Am I now trying to win the approval of men, or of God? Or am I trying to please men? If I were still trying to please men, I would not be a servant of Christ." When we tailor what we do and say just to please people, we fail to please God. Paul understood what David was learning. Sometimes pleasing God means that people won't be impressed. The question is, who do we most want to please, God or people?

If I am worshiping in a church where (to use the example from David's life) dancing in the aisles is normative, I can express my worship in dance and no one will notice—except God! However, if I am attending a church service where this kind of expressiveness is totally foreign, I may choose to limit my dancing activities. If I am sure that my freedom will cause every person gathered to stare at me, I can also be confident that they will no longer be worshiping God, but will be focusing all their attention on me. In this case, I can choose to limit my freedom for the sake of community and the worship of all those gathered.

The apostle Paul addresses this issue of believers choosing to limit their freedom for the sake of community in 1 Corinthians 8. It is a powerful reminder of both our freedom as Christ followers and the wisdom of limiting our freedom for the sake of building community.

LIFE APPLICATION | Worship—Who Is on the Throne?

Throughout this message you will ask the same question as a refrain: "Who is on the throne?" The primary focus of this message will answer the question, "Who is on the throne of David's heart?" This is quickly applied to the hearts of all those gathered.

When David is dancing through the streets, worshiping God with all his might, who do you think is on the throne of his heart at that moment? Is it God or David? It seems obvious that God is on the throne of David's heart. That's all David sees as he worships God with all his might.

When you gather with other followers of Christ to worship or when you worship God throughout the week, who is on the throne of your heart? Are you more concerned about what people may think or say, or is God on the throne of your worship? Is your worship more about how you feel and the experiences you have, or what God receives as you exalt him and lift him up?

CREATIVE MESSAGE IDEA | See the Throne

There is a refrain that runs through this message. We will be asking the question, *Who is on the throne?* It would be helpful to have a throne or large throne-looking chair on the stage area. This can be used as a focal point and visual reminder that someone or something will be on the throne of each person's life.

You will need:

- One large chair or throne-like area on the stage area where you will be preaching or teaching. Be as creative as you like. You could even have a few people who have skills in decorations help set this up.

David gives us a model of fully abandoned worship. God is before his eyes. God is on the throne of his heart. David is lost in worship. We can worship in a similar way, with God fully on the throne of our hearts.

3. Learning from David: Relationships

NARRATIVE ON THE TEXT | Actions of Grace

Mephibosheth is brought before David, the most powerful man in the land, and he bows down to him. What might have been going through Mephibosheth's mind? He knows that his grandfather tried to kill David and that new kings often slaughtered the family members of old kings. When he bows his head before David, there is a chance it will be the last thing he ever does. All his life, he has lived in exile. Now, he is brought before his grandfather's successor.

The words David speaks undoubtedly shock him and many of those gathered. David says, "Don't be afraid . . . for I will surely show you kindness for the sake of your father Jonathan. I will restore to you all the land that belonged to your grandfather Saul, and you will always eat at my table" (2 Samuel 9:7). David takes what has rightfully become his, and he gives it to this outcast man who could have easily been seen as an enemy. David extends grace and gives gifts to this man. David even goes so far as to invite Mephibosheth to dine at the royal table for the rest of his life!

> **SIGNIFICANT SCRIPTURE**
>
> 2 Samuel 9

HISTORICAL CONTEXT | Looking for Family

In 2 Samuel 9 David does something that was not uncommon for kings to do in those days. He goes out hunting for any of Saul's blood relatives. In those days, when a new king took the throne, he would scour the land to find any living relatives of the previous monarch. Then, he would gather all of these people together and kill them! These people represented a challenge, or threat, to the throne. Running through the veins of these relatives was the blood of the previous king, and killing them was a form of job security.

When David becomes king and asks for an inventory of any living relatives of Saul, it seems clear what is coming next. But what David does will be remembered forever! What he does can only happen when God is dwelling on the throne of someone's heart. David is seeking the relatives of Saul (the king who vowed to kill him and who tried to pin David to the wall with a spear) so that he can honor and bless them!

David is not searching for Saul's relatives to exact vengeance but to extend mercy and grace. Second Samuel 9:3

says, "The king asked, 'Is there no one still left of the house of Saul to whom I can show God's kindness?' Ziba answered the king, 'There is still a son of Jonathan; he is crippled in both feet.'" David desires to show mercy to a relative of the man who has chased him like a criminal through the desert.

"'Where is he?' the king asked. Ziba answered, 'He is at the house of Makir son of Ammiel in Lo Debar.' So King David had him brought from Lo Debar, from the house of Makir son of Ammiel" (9:4-5). In verse 6, we find the last existing relative of Saul. His name is Mephibosheth.

INTERPRETIVE INSIGHT | ## Extending Mercy

Does David's compassion and care for Mephibosheth remind you of anyone? Isn't that what God does for you and me? He invites us into his home. Though we are strangers and aliens to God, he invites us in to be a part of his family, to share in his wealth, and to sit at his table. What an incredible image of God we have in David. When David extends mercy to Mephibosheth at every meal, when he looks across the table and sees Saul's grandson, who do you think is on the throne of David's heart?

LIFE APPLICATION | ## Relationships—Who Is on the Throne?

When you see David extending amazing grace and mercy to Mephibosheth, who is on the throne of his heart? God is clearly on the throne and ruling David's life at this time. Only God's mercy and only God's kindness can do that.

The heart of God can beat within us too. When God is on the throne of our heart, we can extend compassion, grace, and generous kindness. Each of us needs to learn to look at our relationships through the eyes of the God whose name is compassion, becoming like Jesus who blessed and prayed for those who nailed him to the cross.

Who in your life does not deserve mercy but needs it? How may God call you to treat this person? What can you do to show that God is on the throne of your relational life?

SIGNIFICANT SCRIPTURE

2 Samuel 11

4. Learning from David: Temptation

NARRATIVE ON THE TEXT | ## Temptation

Up to this point in David's career, everything is going incredibly well. The kingdom is expanding. He is known as one of the greatest kings ever. But in

CREATIVE MESSAGE IDEA | ## Say It Loud!

The only relative of Saul that David can find is Mephibosheth. This is a son of David's dear friend Jonathan. We are also told that Mephibosheth is crippled in both of his feet. Now, just so you will remember this important biblical name, you are all going to say "Mephibosheth" together.

As a leader, first pronounce the name for everyone. Be sure you get it right. If you are not sure of the pronunciation, it is on the copy of the message included in your OTC kit.

If you want to have a little fun, ask everyone to say "Mephibosheth" on the count of three. Count: one, two, three . . . and then when everyone says Mephibosheth, you respond by saying, "God bless you!"

2 Samuel 11 things begin to shift. This story is familiar to many, but it may be new to some. We begin to see the downfall of King David. Although he is a man after God's own heart and God's chosen one to lead Israel, David is also susceptible to the pitfalls of temptation.

Things have begun to change in David's heart. This throne is up for grabs. David, the king of Israel, the most powerful man in all of the region, the one who has been blessed with everything he's ever wanted, begins to desire more. Despite all he has been given, he wants what is not his—what he should never have.

David notices Bathsheba, a beautiful woman, bathing a couple of rooftops over from the palace. He sends his servants to bring her to the palace. David is clearly warned that she is the wife of Uriah the Hittite. It is important to know that Uriah is one of David's most faithful warriors. He is named among David's legendary thirty mighty men (1 Chronicles 11:41). He was with David during his desert years and had served the king and fought at his side.

Knowing all of this, David still brings her to the palace and sleeps with her. It is hard to imagine how incredibly unromantic this scene is. The king sees what he wants and treats her like a food item on a menu or some trinket he sees in the marketplace. He simply says, "I want her. Bring her to me." Then, in one moment of temptation and weakness, David changes the course of his life. He has sexual relations with Bathsheba and sends her home. He dishonors God, shames Bathsheba, and breaks relationship with Uriah, one of his most faithful servants.

Soon Bathsheba realizes she is pregnant and that David is the father. Uriah cannot be the father because he is off fighting in David's war. In response to the news of Bathsheba's pregnancy David concocts a plan to cover his tracks. He tries to convince Uriah to come home and sleep with his wife. But because of Uriah's noble character, he won't do it. Although he comes back to Jerusalem at David's request, he will not go home and enjoy his wife because he is too loyal to his men that are in battle. He will not enjoy a pleasure that they cannot. What painful irony! Uriah has too much integrity to sleep with his own wife while the armies of Israel are at battle, but David had no qualms about sleeping with Uriah's wife and committing adultery.

Since Uriah does not go for David's plan, the king has Uriah killed to cover up his own sin. David actually sends the note that will condemn Uriah to death on the battlefield in Uriah's hand, to be delivered to the commander of Israel's army.

Once Uriah is dead, it seems as if David has gotten away with murder and adultery. In a matter of weeks David, the man after God's own heart, has Bathsheba move in with him as his own wife. David seems to have convinced himself that nothing happened and everything is fine.

It is not temptation itself that grieves God; he is displeased when we give in to temptation.
—CHARLES STANLEY

NEW TESTAMENT CONNECTION

Paradigmatic Laws

The New Testament speaks often about temptation and God's power for us to resist the enticements of the devil. Here are a few passages that speak to this topic:

No temptation has seized you except what is common to man. And God is faithful; he will not let you be tempted beyond what you can bear. But when you are tempted, he will also provide a way out so that you can stand up under it. (1 Corinthians 10:13)

Submit yourselves, then, to God. Resist the devil, and he will flee from you. (James 4:7)

For we do not have a high priest who is unable to sympathize with our weaknesses, but we have one who has been tempted in every way, just as we are—yet was without sin. (Hebrews 4:15)

LIFE APPLICATION | Temptation—Who Is on the Throne?

Now comes the question again: Who do you think is on the throne at this moment of David's life? It is clear that David is ready to take whatever he wants. Temptation comes and he falls for it, hook, line, and sinker! Not only does David fall into this sin, but he spirals downward deeper into deception by trying to cover his tracks. His sin of adultery and cover-up, followed by murder, and the subsequent actions will end up costing David more than he ever dreamed.

When you face temptation, as we all do, who is on the throne? Do you yield to the enticement, or does God's power fill you and allow you to resist? Are you giving in to the same sin over and over? Are you expending large amounts of energy covering your tracks and trying to hide your sin?

When you look at the temptations you face right now, who is on the throne of your life? What causes you to lust and want what is not yours? It is important that we look at the story of David and learn from his experience. He was not satisfied by his sin. It did not end with the one act. David's surrender to temptation began a landslide of sin, deceit, and pain. What a powerful reminder for us to resist the enticement to sin and cling to God's plan for our lives.

5. Learning from David: Confession

INTERPRETIVE INSIGHT | How God Feels About Sin

God is outraged by David's sin. Sometimes we can rationalize our sin and convince ourselves that it is not a big deal. God, however, never looks the other way. He sees David's sin and is ready to deal with it. God sends Nathan to confront the wayward king. Nathan tells David a story about a selfish wealthy man. When David hears how this rich man took a neighbor's pet lamb and slaughtered it to serve a visitor instead of taking a lamb from his own vast flock, he is outraged!

In a shocking twist, Nathan looks at David and says, "You are the man." The prophet then goes on to say

> "This is what the LORD, the God of Israel, says: 'I anointed you king over Israel, and I delivered you from the hand of Saul. I gave your master's house to you, and your master's wives into your arms. I gave you the house of Israel and Judah. And if all this had been too little, I would have given you even more. Why did you despise the word of the LORD by doing what is evil in his eyes? You struck down Uriah the Hittite with the sword and took

his wife to be your own. You killed him with the sword of the Ammonites. Now, therefore, the sword will never depart from your house, because you despised me and took the wife of Uriah the Hittite to be your own.'" (2 Samuel 12:7–10)

SIGNIFICANT SCRIPTURE

2 Samuel 12

INTERPRETIVE INSIGHT | The Ministry of Nathan

Aren't you thankful that God had someone in the kingdom who had enough courage to speak the truth? As king, David could have spoken one word and had Nathan executed. Nathan's willingness to go face-to-face with the king and confront him with his sin is no small task. This is bold and risky.

Nathan is ready to call sin exactly what it is. He does this because he speaks for God and God never sugarcoats sin. Nathan's job is to call David to a higher standard—God's standard. Because of his ministry, David's heart finally breaks over his sin. He comes to a place of humble confession and repentance.

The ministry of Nathan is the call to speak the truth with loving boldness. It is a hard ministry because it puts relationships at risk. Still, it is a ministry we all must be ready to receive. What will you do when God sends a Nathan to call you to repentance and humble confession?

LIFE APPLICATION | Extending and Receiving the Ministry of Nathan

Most of us like to be a Nathan more than we like to hear from a Nathan. We don't mind speaking for God when someone is not living right. We may even have radar that picks up sin in others with great accuracy. If this is the case, we must beware. The ministry of Nathan should be extended with a humble heart and often with tears. We should never take joy in bearing bad news. But if God calls us to speak to another follower of Christ about their sin, we should do this in love and with deep humility.

We also must be ready to receive the ministry of Nathan in our lives. When God sends another believer into our life to raise an issue or uncover a sin, we must be ready to receive this ministry. They have taken a risk by raising an issue in our life. We must be willing to hear their words and then seek God to see if this is his word for us. If it is, repentance is in order.

Is there any place right now, in your life, where someone may be trying to extend the ministry of Nathan and you are stubbornly resistant? Maybe there's somebody you know who needs to hear you speak God's truth into their life. God has put this person on your heart and you are avoiding them like taxes because you don't want to say anything. Just imagine what David's life would have been like if Nathan had said nothing.

NEW TESTAMENT CONNECTION

We think of confession of sins as something private. God sees things differently. Through James, God calls his people to take a posture of mutual confession. The more private we keep our sins, the more likely we are to repeat them! "Therefore confess your sins to each other and pray for each other so that you may be healed. The prayer of a righteous man is powerful and effective" (James 5:16).

SIGNIFICANT SCRIPTURE

Psalm 51

ILLUSTRATION | An Approachable Spirit

In the message that came in the OTC kit, Jarrett tells about a time when someone came to him with a concern. They spoke truth that he needed to hear but did not want to face. However, after they extended the ministry of Nathan, he felt that God had spoken to him in a way that would help him grow as a Christ follower. If you have a story of someone who came to you with the ministry of Nathan, you may want to share it at this time.

INTERPRETIVE INSIGHT | Confession . . .Who Is on the Throne?

When Nathan confronted David, David could have resisted and run. He did not have to confess and repent, but he did. In response to the conviction God brought into David's heart, he wrote Psalm 51. This psalm captures the heart of confession as well as any passage in the entire Bible. In this prayer we hear David admit his sin, face his own weakness, ask for God's forgiveness, and even begin to express hope for how God may still use him to be a blessing to others in the future. Confession gave birth to forgiveness, and forgiveness brought hope alive. Like David, we must learn that confession is often the beginning of a healed and restored relationship with God.

When David finally confesses his sin, when he stops running, when he repents, who is on the throne? Who is on the throne every time we confess from the heart? Who is on the throne when tears of brokenness flow and our heart is bowed before God? The answer is clear: These are the moments that God is on the throne.

PAUSE FOR PRAYER

A Prayer for Nathans

God wants us to extend and receive the ministry of Nathan far more than we do. Take time to pray in two distinct directions:

· Pray for hearts that are humble and receptive to those who may come and speak the truth into our lives.
· Pray for courage and humility as God leads you to speak his truth to other followers of Christ.

LIFE APPLICATION | Time to Confess

All of us have times when confession is exactly what we need. Maybe this is a moment that we need to pray, "Have mercy on me, God, have mercy on me. I've been putting myself on the throne. I have been resistant to you. Have mercy on me."

David desperately needed the ministry of Nathan to wake him up, to get him off of the throne. All of us need the ministry of Nathan in our lives—people who are willing to speak truth to us. Maybe God is using this message to call you to a point of confession and repentance.

INTERPRETIVE INSIGHT | Who Is Jedidiah?

The truth is, anyone who is in a relationship with God is Jedidiah. You're Jedidiah. I'm Jedidiah. That is our true name. You are the one whom God loves. These are the most precious words we can ever hear. God speaks these words to his own son, Jesus, "This is my Son, whom I love; with him I am well pleased" (Matthew 17:5). All who are followers of Christ can live with this assurance that we are loved by God. Our name is Jedidiah!

LIFE APPLICATION | Write it Down

It may be helpful to write that name down in your Bible. Put it in bold letters: Jedidiah.

Write it on the mirror so that when you wake up, you will see it and be reminded that you are the beloved of the Lord. You may want to put a message on your screen saver at home or work: MY NAME IS JEDIDIAH! If someone asks what it means, let them know that you are the beloved of God, and they can be too, through Jesus Christ.

INTERPRETIVE INSIGHT | Back in the Desert

Later in David's life he ends up in the desert again. His son Absalom mounts a political coup (2 Samuel 15), and David leaves Jerusalem. He flees from his kingdom and from his failure as a father. Once more, David finds himself wandering through the desert, alone again with God. He finds himself right back where God had done some of the most formative and important work in David's heart and life many years before.

Again it is in the desert that God does some of his best work. It is also in the desert David is at his best. As he is refined in the furnace of the desert, David is taught humility and dependence on God, and his priorities come back in line. In the desert, God is put back on the throne of David's life.

"Justification by grace through faith" is the theologian's learned phrase for what Chesterton once called "the furious love of God." He is not moody or capricious; he knows no seasons of change. He has a single relentless stance toward us: he loves us.

—BRENNAN MANNING

WORD STUDY

Jedidiah

The child Bathsheba is carrying dies shortly after birth. But God allows her to become pregnant again, and this time she bears a son. David and Bathsheba name this boy Solomon. He later becomes the king of Israel. But Nathan the prophet comes to them and informs them that God has a special name for this child: Jedidiah. This name means, "Loved by the LORD." What a powerful reminder that God is still with this family. With all they have faced, God chooses to remind them of his love, day after day, by giving this baby boy the name Jedidiah.

LIFE APPLICATION | Don't Run from the Desert

There are a lot of people who are in the desert right now. For some people it took all the strength they have just to gather with God's people to hear this message. You don't have to imagine what it would be like to enter the furnace of the desert because you are living there! Your desert may be the loss of a job, the loss of a spouse, brokenness in a significant relationship, financial turmoil, or some other painful situation. The temptation is to try to run out of the desert as quickly as possible. The desert feels scary, it can hurt, and sometimes you wonder if God is really with you in the desert. What you must realize is that you are never alone in the desert. God is with you. In fact, sometimes God leads us into the desert, because it's in the desert that he does some of his greatest work in us. Today God may be asking you to linger in the desert and invite him to do a new and transforming work in your life.

PAUSE FOR REFLECTION | Is God on the Throne of My Life?

As you draw near the end of this message, give people a couple of minutes for reflection to consider honestly what it would look like for them to put God fully on the throne.

He is the only one who is worthy, the only one who is capable, the only one who has ever been able to rule our hearts. He alone can lead with justice and mercy, freedom and love, truth and grace. He is the King of kings and Lord of lords who deserves to be on the throne.

Invite people to identify any place in their lives where they must put God back on the throne. Encourage them to confess if they have been on the throne in their work life, their relationships, their worship, their response to temptation, their family, or any other area. Finally, take time to invite God back onto the throne in any area where he has been removed.

The Heights and Depths of Prayer

PSALMS 22, 42, 103, 136, 137

The Heart of the
MESSAGE

For over 2,500 years, the book of Psalms has been the prayer book of God's people. There is no greater collection of prayers in the history of humanity. The psalms were the prayer book of Jesus. They have guided the prayers of his followers since the church was formed. The church today needs to continue the rich tradition of letting the psalms form and guide our prayer life.

There are many kinds of psalms, and we will survey these over the next two sessions. In this session we will focus specifically on the heights and depths of prayer. The psalms lead us to the heights of celebration, praise, and worship. They also lead us to prayers of honest lament. In this session we will discover the full range of prayer that God invites and encourages. We will also seek to enter into this full spectrum of prayer.

The Heart of the
MESSENGER

In this session we ask God to help make Psalms our prayer book. We will seek to express joy-filled praise as well as the sorrowful depths of lament. To lead a group (large or small) through this process will only happen if you, as the leader, are ready to express your heart to God on both levels.

Take time to prepare your heart by meditating on some of the psalms of praise (Psalms 99, 103, and 104) and the psalms of lament (Psalms 22, 42, and 69). Ask God to free you to express the heights of praise and depths of sorrow to him in prayer as you prepare to bring this message.

Brief Message
OUTLINE

1. Understanding the Psalms
2. A Look at Hebrew Poetry
3. Psalms of Praise
4. Psalms of Lament

27

1. Understanding the Psalms

INTERPRETIVE INSIGHT | ## Not a Happy Little Devotional Book

The book of Psalms is not a happy little devotional book filled with uplifting thoughts and inspiring words. It is not given so we can read one page quickly every morning to help us start the day with a positive attitude. Many people turn to Psalms hoping to have this kind of experience. They hope every psalm will be a piece of uplifting, inspirational, and devotional literature. About half the time they get what they are looking for. The other half of the time they just might end up disappointed or even confused. If you are looking for a daily devotion that is guaranteed to make you smile, Psalms just might throw you a curve ball!

NARRATIVE ON LIFE | ## From the Heights and the Depths

The book of Psalms does contain some of the most uplifting and encouraging words ever penned. At the same time, it contains some of the most honest and tearful prayers ever lifted up. The psalms range from the heights of joy to the depths of sorrow and contain every emotion in between.

Suppose you wake up one morning and decide to read Psalm 136:1–4. Here is what will greet you:

> Give thanks to the LORD, for he is good.
> *His love endures forever.*
> Give thanks to the God of gods.
> *His love endures forever.*
> Give thanks to the Lord of lords:
> *His love endures forever.*
> to him who alone does great wonders,
> *His love endures forever.*

CREATIVE MESSAGE IDEA | ## Experiencing the Heights and Depths of Prayer

In this session you will take time to sing and pray in the midst of the message. There will be suggestions offered for specific songs, Scripture, and prayer direction, but you can structure this in any way that fits your context. If you have instrumentalists and vocalists who lead the worship time, be sure they are prepared to stay the entire time, especially if you have more than one worship service.

If you want to have a good start to your day, this psalm is the ticket! It brings a positive feeling of celebration, victory, and joy. This is a psalm that will breathe life into your soul.

Suppose the next day you continue your reading and turn to Psalm 137:1–4. This is how your reading will begin:

> By the rivers of Babylon we sat and wept
> > when we remembered Zion.
> There on the poplars
> > we hung our harps,
> for there our captors asked us for songs,
> > our tormentors demanded songs of joy;
> > they said, "Sing us one of the songs of Zion!"
> How can we sing the songs of the LORD
> > while in a foreign land?

This psalm is sung in a minor key by people who are in exile. These are prisoners of war. Their hearts are broken and they are weeping. As you read this psalm you may find yourself saying, "Well, that's not very happy. That doesn't make me feel very good."

But here is the truth of the matter: It is not meant to make you feel good. It is there for you to learn to express your sorrow when you feel oppressed, abandoned, and alone. The beauty of the psalms is that they help us express our hearts no matter where we are in our journey of faith and no matter how we are feeling.

LIFE APPLICATION | I Will Learn to Pray the Psalms

Why are the psalms so broad in their perspective? Why do these prayers embrace so much joy and yet so much pain? Because this is how we experience life. Each day can bring moments of incredible satisfaction, joy, passion, and fulfillment. Then, right next to these moments, we can feel inexpressible heartache and sorrow.

We can wake up one morning feeling happy and peaceful. We are sure it is going to be a wonderful day. By the end of the day, something has happened and our heart is broken. We feel sorrow and must face the reality of the pain in this life.

There are other days we wake up and feel down. We are sure there is no reason to get out of bed. But by the end of the day, God has surprised us with joy. God has shown up in some way and amazed us with his goodness and his grace.

What could possibly prepare us for this kind of expansive life experience? The book of Psalms! This is why the OTC reading includes psalms on a regular basis. We want all those who walk through the OTC to learn to love and pray the psalms. Perhaps commit to read a chapter of Psalms each day, even after the OTC is done. However, when you read them, don't expect a daily dose of happy medicine; just let the psalms speak to your heart, from the heights as well as from the depths, and learn to pray authentically as they teach you.

ILLUSTRATION | Never an Unexpressed Thought

Most of us have experienced the innocent words of a child who has blurted out something and shocked everyone within earshot. Children often speak their mind with no filters at all. Only as they grow older and learn to censor themselves (usually at the prompting of concerned parents) do children adjust what they say. The psalms in the Bible have this same unfiltered, uncensored feeling. It is as if every thought is expressed with no concern for the consequences.

If you have a humorous personal story of a child who expressed some thought or information that should have remained censored, you may want to share it.

NARRATIVE ON LIFE | Sometimes Things Get Messy

Some people who have high administration gifts might wonder, "Why didn't they organize the psalms better? Why didn't they put all the happy ones together, the sad ones together, the mad ones together, and so on?" The psalms are kind of messy because life is messy. A happy day and a sad day sometimes come right next to each other. There are even times we experience a great breadth of emotions on the same day.

The psalms teach us to bring our lives in all their fullness before God in all of his fullness. They teach us to bring our lives with all their messiness, ups and

HISTORICAL CONTEXT | A Specific Kind of Literature

The Bible is filled with many types of literature. Some passages are parables, others are allegory, and still others are letters (or epistles). Some are historical narrative, and others are poetry. It is critical that we identify the kind of literature we are reading in the Bible and understand it accordingly.

Reading Psalms is like reading somebody's personal spiritual journal. That's really the kind of literature this book is. If you have ever kept a personal prayer journal, this will make more sense. The book of Psalms is uncensored, unfiltered, raw expressions of the heart. None of the highs or the lows get flattened out. It takes a poetic form, but the words come from the core of the heart.

downs, before God. Let's face it, our lives are not always tidy. The good news, however, is that God understands.

2. A Look at Hebrew Poetry

NARRATIVE ON THE TEXT | Poetry in the Old Testament

It is important to have some background on the psalms and the structure of Hebrew poetry. All of the psalms are poems and were used as songs in worship, so understanding how Hebrew poetry works is helpful.

In English we recognize much of the poetry that has been written by rhyme. For example, if someone says, "Twinkle, twinkle little **star,** " you may finish the poem with the words: "How I wonder what you **are.**" We all recognize how the words rhyme and identify this as a poem.

Hebrew poetry is not characterized primarily by rhyme or by meter. It is identified by something called *parallelism*. This is when ideas or concepts get expressed in pairs. There are three primary variations of Hebrew parallelism. These can be seen over and over in the psalms and other poetic literature in the Old Testament.

The most basic type is called *synonymous parallelism*. This occurs when two thoughts express the same idea. The second line reinforces and reiterates the message of the first. One great example is found in Psalm 103:1:

> Praise the LORD, O my soul;
> all my inmost being, praise his holy name.

SIGNIFICANT SCRIPTURE

Psalm 103

PAUSE FOR PRAYER

Inviting God into the Mess

God sees us, right where we are, and he loves us. If you have a hard time accepting this truth, remember the words of Romans 5:8, "But God demonstrates his own love for us in this: While we were still sinners, Christ died for us." Sometimes we try to hide the truth about our lives from God. As ridiculous as this may sound, we actually try to keep God from seeing the mess in our lives. What we must do is to invite God into the mess. He invites us to tell him about the fears we hold in our hearts, the anger we nurse, our hidden desires, and all the things we would rather not talk about.

ON THE LIGHTER SIDE | Major and Minor Keys

At the most basic level we can divide the psalms into two different groups. There are hymns (psalms that praise God for his great goodness), and there are laments (psalms that ask God for help in times of difficulty, desperation, or need). You might think of them as psalms in major keys and psalms in minor keys.

At this point you may want to have someone ready to play some minor chords on a keyboard, guitar, or some other instrument. As they play these chords, read a few verses from a psalm of lament. Then, have them play a few major chords and read from a psalm of praise.

31

WORD
STUDY

The Psalms Declare What Is in Our Hearts

In New Testament times the people used the psalms to express what was on their heart. These people knew the psalms well, and when they wanted to express themselves, they would often simply recite the words of Psalms.

In possibly the greatest day in the history of the human race, when Jesus rode into Jerusalem, the people could only express their joy by reciting a psalm. During the triumphal entry, as the people got a little taste of what it would be like to live in the kingdom of God, they grabbed on to the Psalms to help them communicate what they were feeling: "Blessed is the king who comes in the name of the Lord!" (Luke 19:38 from Psalm 118:26).

In the darkest moment of human history, when Jesus hung on the cross and felt utterly abandoned and alone, he used one of the psalms to express his heart. At the only time in all eternity when the Son was estranged from the Father and the fellowship of the Trinity was broken, the only words that could do justice to his pain came from the book of Psalms: "About the ninth hour Jesus cried out in a loud voice, 'Eloi, Eloi, lama sabachthani?'—which means, 'My God, my God, why have you forsaken me?' " (Matthew 27:46 from Psalm 22:1).

The entire Bible is God's Word to us. Part of what is so wonderful about the psalms is that they were written to become our words to God. They tell the story of our lives—not just the happy parts. The book of Psalms includes the highs, the lows, and everything in between.

This is synonymous parallelism. "O my soul" is parallel to "all my inmost being." It's another way of saying the same thing. "Praise his holy name" is another way of saying, "praise the Lord." It's emphasizing the absolute importance of praise.

The second kind of parallelism is called *synthetic parallelism* . That occurs when the second phrase elaborates on or explains the first phrase. Psalm 103:2–5 reads:

> Praise the LORD, O my soul,
>> and forget not all his benefits—
> who forgives all your sins
>> and heals all your diseases,
> who redeems your life from the pit
>> and crowns you with love and compassion,
> who satisfies your desires with good things
>> so that your youth is renewed like the eagle's.

As you read this part of the psalm, you can see how David, the author of this psalm, declares that God should be praised for all of his benefits, and then he goes on to list many of them: who forgives sins, heals diseases, and so much more. The first line sets the stage and the following lines build on it.

The third type of Hebrew parallelism that is common is called *antithetical parallelism*. This occurs when thought one and thought two express opposite ideas or feelings. This type appears quite a bit in the book of Proverbs, but also in the book of Psalms. Here is an example from Proverbs 12:15:

> The way of a fool seems right to him,
>> but a wise man listens to advice.

There is a clear contrast here. A foolish person sees his or her own way as the only way. It seems right to him or her all the time. By contrast, a wise person listens to the advice of others. This type of Hebrew poetic structure gives one perspective and then the opposite. The second line is in contrast to the first.

The coordination of "bless" and "don't forget" expresses a profound truth. Only those who praise do not forget. Forgetting God and turning away from God begins when praise has been silenced.
—CLAUS WESTERMANN

3. Psalms of Praise

NARRATIVE ON LIFE | Made to Praise

Praise of God is different from praise that humans may look for. God deserves our worship and adoration. He is worthy of all our praise—and even more than we can give. Heaping praise on God is never wrong because he is God!

Furthermore, we were made to praise him. We are most content and happy when we are doing what we were made to do. Birds fly, it is natural for them. Otters frolic. Plants grow and produce fruit. These things are not shocking; it is the natural order of things. People were made to praise God and give him worship.

ILLUSTRATION | Praise Is Natural

If you have ever stood at the edge of Niagara Falls or seen the Grand Tetons, you understand how natural praise can be. Nobody has to tell you to say, "Ohhh!" and "Ahhhh!" It just comes out. If you have ever watched a professional or Olympic athlete break a record or make a game-winning shot, no one had to tell you to cheer or clap, it just happens. We burst into celebration and praise when we see, hear, or even taste something that is praiseworthy.

If we cannot express our wonder and affirmation, we feel cheated. It leaves us feeling empty. There is something God has placed within us that makes us erupt in praise.

ILLUSTRATION | Love Expresses Itself

Imagine a single man who meets a beautiful single woman. They notice each other. They begin to build a relationship. They fall in love. He is filled with admiration for her character and beauty. Do you think he wants to express it? Do you think she wants him to express it? If he is going to put his feeling of admiration and celebration into words, who should hear them first?

The answer is her!

> *There's something about life and human nature that when you see something that's praiseworthy or admirable, our instinct is to express adoration.*
> —C. S. LEWIS

ON THE LIGHTER SIDE | Seeking Praise

John Ortberg tells the story of when his daughters were young. Sometimes when he was tucking them in at night, he would sit on the side of the bed and ask them, "Who's the smartest, strongest, handsomest, most charming, most wonderful man in the whole world?" They would pause and finally smile and say, "Santa Claus," or, "the Easter Bunny," or some handsome movie star. They would laugh about it because little children understand that you don't pander to somebody's ego needs. It is just not right to heap praise on someone who is out looking for it.

It is natural for this man to express his feelings of love. In the same way, it would be right for her to express what she feels in her heart. When it comes to human relationships, we don't want to express our praise in some general sense. We want to express it to the right person. If that person receives the praise and takes joy in it, that's the best! When this happens, we know what it means. The relationship is reciprocal, and we can begin giving and receiving love and joy together.

INTERPRETIVE INSIGHT | Praise Completes Us!

When we as human beings encounter God, we must express praise, in the same way as a young couple in love express admiration for each other. When we see that God is all-wise, infinitely powerful, eternal, utterly holy, all-loving, completely merciful, inexhaustibly patient, ceaselessly creative, beautiful, and joy-filled, adoration erupts. It is the natural response. Our experience with God will never be complete until we express the praise, wonder, and adoration that is in our hearts. Moreover, it can't be some general expression to whoever is listening; it must be lifted to God directly.

When we express our love to God and when we know he receives and delights in our praise, nothing compares. It just doesn't get any better. That is when we know we're in a relationship with him of reciprocal joy, giving and receiving honor and delight. That is why praise is so important in the life of a follower of Christ.

CREATIVE MESSAGE IDEA | Say It Out Loud

At this point in the message it might make sense to pause and make time for people to respond in praise. You can have people do this silently, but you can also invite corporate expressions of praise.

- First, ask people to write down two or three words that express their praise to God.
- Second, invite them to lift up silent prayers of praise to God.
- Third, ask if there are a few people who would like to stand and express a short word of adoration to God. Encourage others to agree in their heart as members of the family give word to their praise.

If you want to give a little more direction, you could read the following words:

Take a moment and write down two or three words that express who God is to you. The focus is not what he has done for you but on who God is . . . his character. Maybe you find yourself focusing on his holiness, forgiveness, power, or tender mercy. Take a moment quietly before the Lord and write down two or three words that express who God is. Then tell him how you feel. Express these words to God just between you and him. Take a moment to praise him for his qualities, for his attributes.

If you feel it will be appropriate in your worship context, invite a few different people to say a word or sentence prayer out loud to express who God is to them.

NARRATIVE ON THE TEXT | Called to Worship

Psalms of praise have two basic parts. The first part—and it is in most of the praise psalms—is the call to worship. This is the invitation for God's people to enter into his presence and to express their praise to him. Psalm 103 begins:

> Praise the LORD, O my soul;
>> all my inmost being, praise his holy name.
> Praise the LORD, O my soul,
>> and forget not all his benefits—

In a sense the psalmist is calling himself to worship. Before he invites anyone else to worship, he invites himself. Listen to the words, "Praise the LORD, O *my* soul." At the end of Psalm 103 he calls others to worship:

> Praise the LORD, you his angels,
>> you mighty ones who do his bidding,
>> who obey his word.
> Praise the LORD, all his heavenly hosts,
>> you his servants who do his will.
> Praise the LORD, all his works
>> everywhere in his dominion.

David throws open the doors and starts inviting angels, the heavenly host, and everyone and everything in creation to come praise the Lord. Then, at the very end of the psalm, in one final phrase, he comes back to himself with a final invitation to his own soul ("Praise the LORD, O my soul"). The call to worship is a critical and important part of worship.

LIFE APPLICATION | Calling Yourself to Worship

Like David, we need to call ourselves to worship. In the morning we can echo David's prayer and say:

> Praise the LORD, O my soul;
>> all my inmost being, praise his holy name.
> Praise the LORD, O my soul,
>> and forget not all his benefits.

Then we can do exactly that, all day long.

We also need to take seriously the need to call ourselves to worship when we are getting ready to gather with God's people. It used to be that people came early to church; they entered the place of worship in advance of the service so they could prepare their hearts and souls to meet with God among his people. Now we tend to rush into church at the last minute. For some people, their only real

SIGNIFICANT SCRIPTURE

Psalm 103

consistent preparation is getting a cup of coffee into their system before the service starts.

Why not get a good night of rest the day before worship as part of your personal preparation? You might want to make a point of arriving early so you can pray and prepare. You can use the drive time to pray silently or even out loud with others in the car. If you know the passage you will be studying as a congregation, you might want to read it in advance. Get creative in finding ways to call yourself to worship and prepare to meet with God.

NARRATIVE ON THE TEXT | ## Reasons for Worshiping God

In addition to a call to worship, psalms of praise simply list and expound reasons God is worthy of praise. Some psalms will focus on one attribute and develop it. Others will give a number of qualities of God. There's an interesting example of this in Psalm 103:15–17:

> As for man, his days are like grass,
>   he flourishes like a flower of the field;
> the wind blows over it and it is gone,
>   and its place remembers it no more.
> But from everlasting to everlasting
>   the LORD's love is with those who fear him,
>   and his righteousness with their children's children.

This is also an example of antithetic parallelism. There is a contrast of human beings, whose days are numbered, and God, who is everlasting. Human beings are finite, God is eternal.

There is an interesting variation in this passage. We are reminded that the days of people are like grass; they are limited. We would then expect the psalmist to say, "As for God, his days are eternal, from everlasting to everlasting." But he doesn't. What the psalmist says is, God's *love* is everlasting.

David is overwhelmed by both the eternal existence of God and God's everlasting love. It never ends. You never get to the bottom of it. How can you

ON THE LIGHTER SIDE | ## Time Flies

The psalmist notices that the years of a person are like the flower of the field. In other words, time flies. Our life begins, and before we know it so many years have passed. Have you ever noticed how fast life goes? Have you ever noticed how fast you are aging? If not, just ask the person next you. They have noticed!

not want to worship a God like that? The reality of God's love moves David to express praise and delight. This is the heart of worship.

NARRATIVE ON LIFE | ## Worship and Music

There is an important distinction that we all need to understand. The essence of worship is *not* great music. Sometimes people talk about worship as if it's synonymous with music. It's not. Worship is not primarily about getting to hear music that I like. Worship is not about having an emotional experience. It is also not simply about showing up at a church and making it through the service. Sometimes people go to a service of worship, a corporate gathering of Christ followers, and their focus is on, "Can I feel what I want to feel?" That's not the heart of worship. Sometimes God gives gifts of great joy or great emotion in worship, but that is not the heart of it. Worship is so much more than any of this.

INTERPRETIVE INSIGHT | ## The Heart of Worship

The heart of worship is to delight in the goodness, greatness, and glory of God. It is to reflect deeply on his character and attributes and then to respond in natural praise and adoration. We then express this directly to him, and we know he receives it. Worship is to reflect on God with our mind, our will, and our heart in a way that moves us to delight in him and then to be overwhelmed when we realize that he also delights in us, far more than we ever dreamed.

> *To worship is to quicken the conscience by the holiness of God, to feed the mind with the truth of God, to purge the imagination by the beauty of God, to open the heart to the love of God, to devote the will to the purpose of God.*
> —WILLIAM TEMPLE

CREATIVE MESSAGE IDEA | ## Worship Together

Note: Watch the video supplied with this kit here.

Before you begin looking at the psalms of lament, plan to have a time of praise and celebration. Invite people to meet with God and express their praise and adoration in a number of ways.

Small Groups

You can have people get into small groups of three or four and offer up short prayers of praise. Those who feel more comfortable praying on their own should feel free to do this. This particular kind of expression in praise fits best in a context where most of the people gathered are already believers.

Corporate Worship

Plan a time of singing together. Have a praise team ready to lead. Some possible songs might be:

- "Shout the Name of Jesus," by Matt Shepardson
- "Sweet Presence of Jesus," by Tommy Walker
- "All Creatures of Our God and King," by Francis of Assisi
- "Doxology," by Thomas Ken
- "Holy, Holy, Holy," by Reginald Heber

NARRATIVE ON LIFE | Unmanaged Faces

Dallas Willard says, "One of the things that we love about children is they have not learned to manage their faces. Whatever is going on in a child's heart is just right there on their face. There's joy on the face of a child when there's joy in their heart."

As we grow up we learn to manage our faces carefully. Yet, God wants us to praise him with an unmanaged face. We can learn to express our praise to God with our words and faces. It may be helpful for many of us to rediscover the free expressions of childhood when it comes to our worship.

4. Psalms of Lament

INTERPRETIVE INSIGHT | Prayers from the Depths

The psalms of lament are a much different psalm from the praise psalm. These are recorded in the Bible to help us learn how to pray this way also. Just as God invites and gladly receives our prayers of praise, he also welcomes and blesses us for our prayers of lament.

Many people might say, "I don't think I know how to lament. I am not sure what a lament really is." Well, here are some questions:

- Do you know how to complain?

- If your body is aching, do you know how to groan?

- When hard times come, do you ever shed tears of sorrow?

- When people treat you unfairly, do you ever tell God that you don't understand?

If you answered yes to any of these questions, you already know something about laments.

A lament psalm is basically a complaint. It is an honest and heartfelt expression of pain, sadness, and brokenness. Interestingly, the psalms of lament are the largest single category in the whole book of Psalms.

NARRATIVE ON THE TEXT | Tears and a Broken Heart

As we read Psalm 42, we begin to understand the heartbeat of a lament. Listen to these words and see if you can identify with this kind of psalm. Read Psalm 42:1–6 and 9. Can you feel the pain? Can you hear the despair? Can you sense honest complaint coming through? The psalmist holds nothing back:

• My only food, day and night, is my tears.

• Other people are taunting me because it seems God will not deliver.

• I used to gather with God's people for worship, now I can't. My joy and thanksgiving are gone.

• My soul is downcast and disturbed.

• I feel forgotten by God.

• I am oppressed by my enemies.

These are not the statements of someone at the top of his spiritual game. This is a far cry from the celebration of Psalm 103. Yet this is a prayer that is pleasing to God. When was the last time you dared pray with this kind of bold honesty?

NARRATIVE ON LIFE | The Laments Are for Us

The psalms of lament deal with a number of areas of struggle, though they tend to be somewhat general. There are few details in Psalms, and this is intentional on the part of the psalmists. The psalms were written to be all-purpose prayers. They can be used by people in many various situations. The beauty of these psalms is that we can adapt them to our unique needs. We can use them to give voice to what's happening in our lives and hearts.

NARRATIVE ON THE TEXT | The Content of Laments

The laments can help us when we face any kind of pain or time of struggle. However, there are four primary topics that are addressed in the laments.

The fear of enemies. In the laments we hear people crying out to God because they are being attacked by an enemy. Enemies can take many shapes and forms. Usually in the psalms they were people attacking the psalmist physically or perhaps emotionally. The psalmist was seeking relief or deliverance from such individual(s).

For you, an enemy could be your boss, a neighbor, a coworker, or everybody on the freeway. It could even be somebody you usually love but are facing conflict with at this time. It could be somebody you are sitting near in church, even the person next to you. Your enemy could be depression, loneliness, fear, or sin. It's whatever or whoever you need deliverance from. God invites you to come to him and cry out for strength to resist the attack you are under today.

The battle with illness. A second category in the laments is the problem of sickness. This can be a physical problem or even the stress you feel due to the burdens of life. Anything that creates stress and pain in your body is included in this kind of lament.

NEW TESTAMENT CONNECTION

The Hope of Resurrection

When we come to a place where we have to face the reality of death, it is critical that we remember that death is not the end for followers of Christ. We need to be free to lament and express our fear, anger, and sense of loss. At the same time, we must keep in mind the truth that those who die in Christ have an eternal inheritance that nothing, including death, can ever take away. Read 1 Corinthians 15 to see what Paul says about the assurance we can have if we are followers of Christ.

PAUSE FOR REFLECTION

Identifying My Pain

Provide time for everyone gathered to take a few moments, privately between themselves and God, to lift up prayers of lament. We all have some area where we have a deep need for God's help. Encourage each person to think through the four topics that come up often in prayers of lament and identify where they are feeling pain, hurt, fear, or just a sense of being stuck.

Here's the truth about us: We carry things in our bodies all day. We can be anxious about a test in school, fearful about a work review coming up, or tense about a broken relationship. These things impact our bodies. Maybe we are facing financial pressures or are worried about a child who is making poor choices. We might be walking around with churning stomachs, stiff necks, aching heads, sweaty palms, and boiling blood. We all know exactly what the psalmist means when he says, "My bones suffer."

In a sense, God is using your body to tell you to pray. Laments are a way to tell God how you are feeling and to cry out for help. Life in this fallen world brings so much more than we were ever intended to handle on our own. Thus, our physical sickness, pain in our bodies, and emotional turmoil are all opportunities to pray.

The reality of death. The sense of pressure or trouble is often so severe in the psalms of lament that the psalmist speaks of being at the point of death. When the psalmists talk about Sheol (NIV "grave"), one idea behind this term is that they don't see any way out. Death becomes a picture of a life that feels hopeless and a soul that is in mortal agony.

Of course there are also times when a lament is about more than fear of death or a sense of utter hopelessness. There were times when the psalmist was under attack and genuinely fearful for his life. Sometimes a prayer of lament will be lifted up by a person who is on the edge of death because of an illness or even old age. The reality of death can bring us to a place of honest prayer.

The anxiety of being trapped. The fourth and final category in the laments is the anxiety of being trapped. Through the psalms of lament we find images like drowning or being stuck in a pit. The idea is that we all know how it feels to be stuck in a situation we can't seem to get out of. In our prayer of lament we might cry out to God and say, "I'm stuck in a financial pit and I can't get out." We might call out to God because we feel trapped in a painful marriage, habitual sin, destructive relational patterns, or some kind of addiction. In a lament we call to God, admit that we are stuck, and ask him to help get us out of our situation.

INTERPRETIVE INSIGHT | Affirmation of Praise

Although the laments do have the feeling of a complaint, they are unique in that they almost always have a feeling of hope. Even in the deepest pits of despair, the psalmist seems to have an unquenchable spirit of hope. Bernhard W. Anderson, in his classic book, *Out of the Depths (The Psalms Speak for Us Today)*, writes:

> The term "lament" is not an altogether satisfactory label for these psalms. The word may suggest a pessimistic view of life, a "bemoaning of a tragedy which cannot be reversed." But this is not the mood of the psalmists. What characterizes these psalms, with very few exceptions, is the confidence that the situation can be changed if Yahweh wills to intervene.

What a great reminder that even in the most painful and difficult times, God's people can cling to hope.

PAUSE FOR PRAYER

Seeking God's Comfort

Take a moment to pray for all of those gathered. You may want to prepare your own prayer or use the one provided below:

Heavenly Father, you hear every prayer. You know every heart. You count every tear. You know, God, that we have a desperate need for you. You know, Father, the stories of all of the men and the women in this room who will not make it if you don't help them. In this moment, because you ask us to, as your people have done for thousands of years, we place before you our heaviest burdens, our biggest worries, and our darkest fears. We cry out to you and seek you for the help that only you can offer. We do this trusting that you are the God who listens and cares for his people. In Jesus' name we pray, Amen.

The Greatest Prayers of All Times

PSALM 19, 30, 51, 58, 96, 103, 119, 137

The Heart of the
MESSAGE

In this message we will look at five different kinds of psalms. Each of these categories helps us speak our heart to God in new and powerful ways. We will practice making the psalms our prayer to God. God longs for us to learn to pray in deeper and richer ways, and one of the best tools we have for developing our prayer life is the book of Psalms.

As we learn from the psalms and as they become part of our very hearts, we will grow. The psalms will enable us to give voice to our thanks, sorrow, anger, fear, praise, and so much more. The psalms have been an indispensable tool in the spiritual lives and growth of God's people for thousands of years. We need to let them become ours.

The Heart of the
MESSENGER

Each section of this message holds the key to unlock a part of our heart and express it to God. From the heights of thanksgiving to the raw edge of anger, the psalms help us tell God what we are feeling. From the depths of rebellious shame to the heights of the throne room of God, the psalms will instruct us if we let them. As a leader, take time to let the psalms speak to your heart and prepare you to speak to God. Meditate on the following psalms as you prepare your heart to bring this message to God's people (Psalm 30, 51, 19, and 58).

Brief Message
OUTLINE

1. Thanksgiving Psalms
2. Penitential Psalms
3. Wisdom Psalms
4. Imprecatory Psalms
5. Enthronement Psalms

NARRATIVE ON LIFE | How Do We Teach Prayer?

How do you teach someone to pray? Jesus' disciples came to him and said, "Lord, teach us to pray." All followers of Christ have a desire to learn how to pray in authentic ways. Where do we look to find tools to develop our prayer lives?

Many parents have grappled with this question and have developed standardized ways to teach their children to pray. Often it looks something like this. You learn to pray by talking to God each night before bed. Kneel next to the bed, fold your hands, close your eyes, and say:

> Now I lay me down to sleep,
> I pray thee, Lord, my soul to keep.
> If I should die before I wake,
> I pray thee, Lord, my soul to take.
> God bless. . . . [At this point you list as many people as come
>   to mind.]
> [Then you finish with a declarative] Amen!

Is there anything wrong with this approach to teaching prayer? No. It is a great starting point for children. It is also helpful to teach some basic prayers that can be offered before a meal or at a time of need. But, if a follower of Christ gets to be twenty, thirty, or fifty and that is the entire sum of his or her prayer life, he or she has missed the breadth, beauty, and power of prayer. There is so much more, and the book of Psalms is the best guide to help us navigate the rich and varied landscape of prayer.

1. Thanksgiving Psalms

INTERPRETIVE INSIGHT | Thanksgiving Psalms

SIGNIFICANT SCRIPTURE

Psalm 30

Psalm 30 is one of the greatest psalms of thanksgiving in the Bible. Invite those gathered to read the first five verses with you.

Psalms of thanksgiving explode with celebration for what God has done. In the last session we looked at psalms of praise that focus on who God is. The direction of those psalms was God's character and attributes. Psalms of thanksgiving shift our attention to the mighty acts of God and all he does for his children. God has been good, beyond description. The psalms of praise help release the thanks that are locked up in our heart. They remind us that God is worthy of being thanked for all of his mighty deeds.

ILLUSTRATION | What Do You Say?

It is a short sentence, only two words. The entire declaration is only two syllables, but it is so hard to learn. The sentence is, "Thank you!" Why is it so hard to learn these two words?

Every parent discovers that part of their job is to ask each child, over and over again, "What do you say?" When a meal is served, they ask their daughter, "Honey, what do you say?" When a gift is received from grandparents, they prompt their son, "Danny, what do you say?" When a neighbor has given them a ride home from school, they ask them, "What do you say?" Over and over, year after year, parents ask their children this question countless times in a variety of ways.

Why do parents do this? Because thanksgiving is an appropriate response to someone's kindness. Parents ask this question again and again, longing for the day when their son or daughter will say it on their own. What joy fills a mother's heart when her son gives a smile and says, "Thanks, Mom!" all on his own.

NARRATIVE ON LIFE | Remember God's Goodness

We need to learn to remember how good God has been to us. We have admitted our need and cried out to him on many occasions. In response, God has heard our cry and responded in powerful ways. Now we need to respond with heartfelt thanks.

How have you cried to God and seen him work on your behalf?

• Maybe you needed healing and God came and touched you.

• Maybe you had financial needs at some point and God was generous.

• Maybe you were sad, or you were in deep pain, and God gave you comfort.

HISTORICAL CONTEXT | Ancient Covenants

There is a basic structure or movement in the psalms of thanksgiving. They follow this basic format:

1. **An admission of need.** The psalmist will declare an awareness that he was in a time of need. This can be a specific need or something general, but there is an expression of need lifted up to God.

2. **A cry to God.** Next, the psalmist declares that he cried out to God in his time of need. He made his need known and trusted in God to protect, provide, deliver, or meet his need in some other way.

3. **An expression of thanks for God's work.** Finally, the psalmist identifies the way that God heard his prayer and acted. Then, a natural and joy-filled expression of thanksgiving follows. This prayer of thanks is always rooted in what God has done and how his mighty power has been revealed.

- Maybe you felt useless and God showed you that you have distinct gifts that he wants to use for his glory.

- Maybe you felt alone and God sent you a friend.

- Maybe you were anxious and God gave you hope.

Whatever God has done, the appropriate response is thanksgiving.

NARRATIVE ON LIFE | Giving a Joyful Offering

During your time of singing you may want to receive the offering. If you do, take a moment and talk about how the giving of offerings is really a response of thankfulness. When we give with joy in our hearts, we are acknowledging that God has been so good to us, he has provided all we have, and we are glad to give back to him. The offering is not an interruption in our worship service. It is an act of worship, and especially it is an act of thanksgiving. It's a way of saying to God, "Thank you that you've blessed me with so much. I want to give this to you as an expression of my gratitude."

CREATIVE MESSAGE IDEA | Put It on Paper

Take time as a group to write a short psalm or prayer of thanksgiving. Use the basic structure we find in the psalms of thanksgiving. Invite all those gathered to experience what it feels like to be a psalmist. Even those who are not fond of writing should be encouraged to participate.

After a short time for writing, you may want to invite a few people to stand and read their psalm of thanksgiving.

You will need:

- Half sheets of paper that have the basic structure of thanksgiving psalms (admission of need, cry to God, response of thanksgiving) printed on them.
- If you meet in a large room, you may need some microphones set up so people can use them to read their psalms of thanksgiving.

CREATIVE MESSAGE IDEA | Lifting Up Our Thanks

After people have written their psalms of thanks and some have read them, plan to lift your voices together in songs of thanks. There are many songs of thanks that are appropriate. Some possible songs you could use are:

- "For the Beauty of the Earth," by Folliott Pierpoint
- "Now Thank We All Our God," by Martin Rinkart
- "For All That You've Done, I Will Thank You," by Dennis L.

Jernigan

- "Give Thanks," by Henry Smith
- "I'm Forever Grateful," by Mark Altrogge
- "Better Is One Day," by Matt Redman
- "I Could Sing of Your Love Forever," by Martin Smith
- "Mourning into Dancing," by Tommy Walker

LIFE APPLICATION | Remember to Say Thank You!

Just as children need to hear parents ask them, "What do you say?" we also need to be reminded to be thankful. The truth is, sometimes we forget. We get busy, we become selfish, or we just get used to God's goodness and don't notice how much he does for us.

Commit to grow as a person of thankfulness. Remember to say thank you. Here are two ideas for growing in thankfulness:

Daily reminders. Use the things that come up every day as thanksgiving prompters. Here are some ideas of things that can remind you to pause and lift up thanks to God:

- when you wake up in the morning

- each time you have a meal

- whenever you hear someone complain (including yourself!)

- each time you hear a bird chirp, a dog bark, or a cat meow

- when a baby cries

- when you hit a green light (and when you hit a red light)

- when someone smiles at you (and when someone scowls)

- when you lay your head on the pillow at the end of the day

Identify specific things that happen regularly in your day and use these as thanksgiving prompters.

Do a life inventory. Plan a time when you will get thirty or more minutes free of interruptions. Start from your childhood and begin identifying times you have seen a need in your life, cried to God, and watched him answer. Each time you identify a life situation where God moved on your behalf, write it down. Write just a few words to remind you what God did and when he did it. Then spend a few moments saying thank you.

Some of the things you will remember may have evoked great thanks in your life back when they happened. In other cases you may realize that you never really thanked God for his goodness and provision at that time of your life. In either case, use this as an opportunity to express the depth of thanks you feel.

Then, move on in your life and continue the same process. Here is a helpful way to walk through your life:

- my birth to my toddler years (you probably don't remember, but others may have told you stories of God's goodness to you, even before you were born)

NEW TESTAMENT CONNECTION

A Cheerful Giver

In 2 Corinthians 9:6–8 we read:

Remember this: Whoever sows sparingly will also reap sparingly, and whoever sows generously will also reap generously. Each man should give what he has decided in his heart to give, not reluctantly or under compulsion, for God loves a cheerful giver. And God is able to make all grace abound to you, so that in all things at all times, having all that you need, you will abound in every good work.

Our attitude in giving should be one of cheer and joy. Our giving should be generous and willing. How can this be? In hard economic times, when we work so hard for what we have, when giving to God means that we have less, how can we be joyful? Because giving is a great way we express thankfulness. God is the one who is able to give us grace and all the resources we need. Our generous and thankful offerings are a declaration that we understand that every good thing we have in this life is a gift from God's hand (James 1:17).

- my childhood

- my teenage years (think of all the potential dangers God saved you from—sometimes without your even asking!)

- my young adult years

- my middle age years

- my elderly years

2. Penitential Psalms

INTERPRETIVE INSIGHT | Penitential Psalms

SIGNIFICANT SCRIPTURE

Psalms 51 and 103

Another category of psalms are called penitential psalms. They help us to learn how to do self-examination and how to express confession to God. They are open and honest prayers where we say, "Lord, in the light of your goodness, in the light of your glory, I see myself as I really am. I have got to say, I am sorry. I have sinned. I have wronged you. I have broken your heart." These psalms give voice to our sorrow over sin, and they also move us to a place of repentance and transformed lives.

ILLUSTRATION | The Value of Examination

In a sense, the penitential psalms are like X rays that look into us and show where we are broken and where the sickness of sin is hidden. We need these psalms for our souls in the same way we need a regular physical to be sure we are physically healthy.

There is a true story about a couple with a five-year-old daughter. The little girl fell out of a tree and dropped about ten feet to the ground. They rushed her to the hospital to make sure she was not injured. The doctors did X rays and CAT scans to see if there were any broken bones or any internal damage. The good news is that she wasn't damaged by the fall. But, to the surprise of everyone, the tests revealed a brain tumor.

CREATIVE MESSAGE IDEA | Songs of Confession

After a time of silent prayer and reflection, respond together by singing a song of confession. Here are a few ideas:

- "Cleanse Me," by J. Edwin Orr
- "Just As I Am," by Charlotte Elliott

- "Whiter Than Snow," by James Nicholson
- "Come, Let Us Worship and Bow Down," by Dave Doherty
- "You Are Merciful to Me," by Ian White
- "Create in Me—Psalm 51," by Matt Shepardson and Greg Ferguson

The tumor was benign, but it was growing. The doctors did surgery as soon as they could, and it went very well. As a matter of fact, she asked for a cheeseburger the day after surgery! Her life may well have been saved because she fell out of a tree and had unplanned X rays. Those tests revealed what would not have been found otherwise.

On a lighter note, the little girl's mom talks about how she can picture two guardian angels looking over that little girl when she was up in the tree. One of them says to the other one, "You push her." The other one replies, "No, I'm not going to push her. You push her."

NARRATIVE ON LIFE | Examining Our Hearts

We don't have to fall out of a tree to get X rays of our heart and soul. God has given us the penitential psalms to help in this process. It is as if the psalmist is saying, "How can I find out about something that's toxic to my body, that could destroy my soul, paralyze my heart, sear my conscience, and separate me from God, but I can't see it? How do I examine my heart?"

Each time we read these psalms and make them our own, God helps us see where we need to confess and repent. Sometimes we see the sickness growing in our soul. At other times we are blind to it. But always God is ready to reveal it, if we ask, and deal with our sin.

LIFE APPLICATION | Doing Moral Inventory

Pause in the message and invite people to a time of moral inventory. Read some selected verses from Psalm 51 and 103 that you feel will be helpful for those gathered. Then, allow silent time for private reflection and confession.

First, invite God to help in the process of searching our hearts. If we do this on our own, we are likely to miss things and go through the process too fast. Or we can become neurotic and get into all kinds of unhealthy guilt. Self-examination is only safe and right when we do it with God's help.

Question 1: God, please show me my hidden faults! Maybe it's a bad habit, maybe it's an attitude, maybe it's something I've done today or even something that has been hidden for years. It could be a failure to love someone, or perhaps I have avoided speaking the truth. Maybe you have been choosing pain avoidance rather than courage. Whatever it is, ask God to show you.

Question 2: God, send me a Nathan! That is a courageous prayer. When we pray this, we are admitting that there are some areas of darkness in our hearts and lives that we know we can't deal with on our own. Maybe we can't see the sin. Or perhaps we see it and feel God's conviction, but can't seem to stop. It could be that we need a brother or sister to come alongside of us and help us in the process of turning from our sin.

PAUSE FOR
REFLECTION

Words of Assurance

You may want to give these words of assurance as you close this session of the message:

Regret doesn't get the last word. Sin doesn't get the last word. Guilt does not get the last word. *You are forgiven.* As far as the east is from the west, that's how far God has removed your transgressions from you. If you have received the forgiveness that comes through a relationship with Jesus Christ, you can be filled with joy right now. This is the good news God has for you. All your sins are gone, and you are loved by God with an everlasting love!

Second, invite people to come before God humbly in these moments with no defensiveness or no stiff necks, but with soft and open hearts. Pray for the convicting ministry of the Holy Spirit to take place in each heart. Acknowledge God's great desire to heal and forgive.

LIFE APPLICATION | **Extending Forgiveness**

Think about David for a moment. After he committed murder, adultery, and a number of other sins, his heart was broken, and he came back to the Lord. He asked God for mercy and compassion. David pleaded with God to blot out his transgressions and wash away all his sin. David realized there was great brokenness in him and that he could not get himself out of the pit he had fallen into. Only God could save him. David also committed to help extend grace to others and to help them turn back to God.

Like David, when we have become aware of the greatness of God's grace toward us, we want to help others know that his grace is available to them as well. We can begin by seeking to have a forgiving heart toward those who have wronged us. The more we understand and accept the forgiveness God offers, the more freely we extend grace to those who have wronged us.

Whom do you have in your life that needs to experience the fullness of God's forgiveness? How might God want to use you as an ambassador of his grace in

CREATIVE MESSAGE IDEA | **Receiving Forgiveness**

Invite everyone to stand before God to receive a reminder of his promise to forgive and cleanse. You may want to ask them to take a posture of receiving in the following way.

Ask them to imagine that they love M&M candies. Ask them how they would put their hands if they knew you were going to pour out as many M&Ms as they could hold. How would they cup their hands together to get the maximum volume of candy? Invite them to hold out their hands in that kind of receiving posture. If they are not a fan of M&Ms, they can imagine you are going to give them as many fresh blueberries (or some other favorite food) as they can hold.

As they stand with hands and hearts ready to receive a reminder of God's grace and power to forgive, read the following passages with bold confidence:

The LORD is compassionate and gracious,
    slow to anger, abounding in love.

He will not always accuse,
    nor will he harbor his anger forever;
he does not treat us as our sins deserve
    or repay us according to our iniquities.
For as high as the heavens are above the earth,
    so great is his love for those who fear him;
as far as the east is from the west,
    so far has he removed our transgressions from us.
As a father has compassion on his children,
    so the LORD has compassion on those who fear him. (Psalm 103:8–13)

If we confess our sins, he is faithful and just and will forgive us our sins and purify us from all unrighteousness. (1 John 1:9)

the life of this person? Are there people you need to forgive as you grow in your understanding of how much God has forgiven you?

3. Wisdom Psalms

INTERPRETIVE INSIGHT | Wisdom Psalms

The wisdom psalms give instruction and guidance to God's people. They praise and celebrate God's law. They rejoice in the pure beauty of the words God has given us in the Scriptures. These psalms are intended to motivate and help us desire to follow the teachings of God's law with all our heart. The most remarkable one of these wisdom psalms is Psalm 119. It has 176 verses, every one of which calls us to delight in God's law.

INTERPRETIVE INSIGHT | The Arrangement of Psalms

There are many ways the psalms were structured by the authors. We already looked at Hebrew poetry, but Psalm 119 introduces a new structure. It is a praise of God's wisdom from the beginning to the end. For this reason, the entire psalm, all twenty-two stanzas, is based on the Hebrew alphabet. Each verse in the first

NEW TESTAMENT CONNECTION

Forgive Us Our Debts

Jesus taught his followers to pray: "Forgive us our debts, as we also have forgiven our debtors" (Matthew 6:12).

It is clear through both the Old and New Testaments that we are to respond with a spirit of forgiveness toward those who have wronged us. There is a relationship between the ways we offer forgiveness and how we will receive it.

ON THE LIGHTER SIDE | Let's Read It Together

Using the Power Point slides provided on the CD-ROM, invite those gathered to read the portion of Psalm 119 as it is printed on the screen (it will be in a very small font—too small to read).

Remind people that this is only a portion of the psalm (which is 176 verses long).

CREATIVE MESSAGE IDEA | In Praise of God's Wisdom

Encourage each person present to open a Bible to Psalm 119 and begin reading anywhere in the psalm. After they have read four to five verses, invite them to do the following:

· Begin circling (if they have their own Bible) all of the varied words that are used as references to God's law (precepts, statutes, teachings, word, decrees, and more).

· Have them see how far they read before they run into something about the power and goodness of God's law.
· Invite them to tell the person next to them one thing they learn about God's law from the verses they read.

section begins with the first letter of the Hebrew alphabet, Aleph. Each verse in the final section begins with the last letter, Taw. This is the author's way of saying that the law of God, his wisdom, is all we need for life; it is all-inclusive!

NARRATIVE ON LIFE | The Power of God's Word

Read the words of Psalm 19:9–11 in unison with those gathered:

> The fear of the LORD is pure,
>> enduring forever.
> The ordinances of the LORD are sure
>> and altogether righteous.
> They are more precious than gold,
>> than much pure gold;
> they are sweeter than honey,
>> than honey from the comb.
> By them is your servant warned;
>> in keeping them there is great reward.

Trouble and Perplexity drive me to prayer; and prayer drives away perplexity and trouble.

—PHILIPP MELANCHTHON, SIXTEENTH CENTURY

This passage, and others in the wisdom psalms, put life into perspective. God's wisdom is more valuable than anything else in the entire world. We don't often see it this way, but it is true. The Hebrews prized the wisdom of God more than any other possession. God's wisdom warns us and keeps us from stumbling. It is the source of truth and blessing.

God longs for us to come to a place where we love his Word and hunger for it. Reading the Word of God and growing in his wisdom is not a chore but a privilege. It is not a burden we bear but a source of amazing strength in the life of a follower of Christ.

LIFE APPLICATION | Making Space for God's Word

If we went for two weeks without eating any food, our bodies would become weak. We would notice it! If we go too long without the food of God's Word and the filling of his wisdom, we become spiritually malnourished. It is critical for God's people to make space in their day to read, study, and meditate on God's Word. This can be first thing in the morning, at a lunch break, in the evening, or at the close of the day. The timing is not as important as the condition of our hearts.

God longs to meet with us and speak into our lives. One of the most powerful ways he does this is through the wisdom of his Word. Each of us should find a time and place where we can spend some uninterrupted moments with God and feed on his truth.

Holy Space

One man found that the best time and place for him to meet with God was over his lunch break. Every day he would go out to his red pickup truck and climb into the cab. He kept his Bible on the dashboard, and he used these moments to meet with God. With a praise tape playing quietly, he would pray and read the Bible. The cab of his truck became a holy space, a sacred meeting place where God met with this follower of Christ.

> **SIGNIFICANT SCRIPTURE**
>
> Psalm 58 and 137

4. Imprecatory Songs

INTERPRETIVE INSIGHT Imprecatory Psalms

In the last session of this study we focused on psalms of lament. Imprecatory psalms are actually a specific kind of lament. These are prayers that deal with the issue of vindication. We might call them, "Get-My-Enemies Laments." In these prayers we hear the psalmist expressing harsh words that sound something like this, "Lord, I feel oppressed by this person, and I would really like you to break all their teeth. Okay?" Some of them get even more graphic. In some of these prayers the psalmist is saying, "God, I am under attack and I am asking you to rain down judgment upon my enemy"!

To get a sense for how severe these psalms could be, listen to these words from Psalm 58:6–8:

> Break the teeth in their mouths, O God;
>> tear out, O Lord, the fangs of the lions!
> Let them vanish like water that flows away;
>> when they draw the bow, let their arrows be blunted.
> Like a slug melting away as it moves along,
>> like a stillborn child, may they not see the sun.

These are harsh words. Nevertheless, they are spoken from an honest and broken heart. Most important, they are expressed to God. Rather than go out and get revenge, the psalmist cries out to God and leaves judgment where it belongs, in the hands of a just God.

NARRATIVE ON LIFE Where Do I Take My Anger?

There is a strange beauty to this kind of prayer. We come to God with a lament of vindication and say, "God, this person has made me so mad, they have hurt me so deeply, all I want to do is get them back. But I won't, Lord. I won't strike out. I leave judgment to you." Do you begin to see the importance of this kind of

> **NEW TESTAMENT CONNECTION**
>
> ## Praying for Our Enemies
>
> For Christ's followers, when we come to words like this, it causes us to stop and wonder: How can I reconcile these words with what Jesus teaches? Jesus said things like Luke 6:27–29:
>
> But I tell you who hear me: Love your enemies, do good to those who hate you, bless those who curse you, pray for those who mistreat you. If someone strikes you on one cheek, turn to him the other also. If someone takes your cloak, do not stop him from taking your tunic.
>
> How does this kind of teaching fit with these psalms? Although scholars debate exactly how to understand the imprecatory psalms, there is a sense that God wants us to bring all of our feelings, including our deepest anger, to him. By bringing it to him, we are deterred from taking it out on those who have made us angry. Also, in his presence, as we pour out all that is in our hearts, he can begin a work of changing our hearts and teaching us how to respond in a manner that honors him.

*Rage belongs before
God.*
—MYRIS LOWHOF

prayer? As harsh as it sounds, it is a powerful prayer because in an imprecatory prayer we are saying, "I won't strike back. I won't raise my hand. I won't return evil for evil. I put it in your hands, Lord. By the way, if you would like to get them for me, that would be just fine!" What a great reminder that we can, and should, come to God with all of our feelings, even anger!

LIFE APPLICATION | Where Do I Go with My Anger?

Where do you go with your anger? There are lots of places we can take our rage, and most of them are terribly destructive. What happens when you take your anger to your spouse or your children? What consequences might this have? Some take their rage out on the road, or they put a fist through a wall. Again, how does this help? Still others carry their anger into the workplace or they take it out on the family pet. Take time to identify where you tend to take out your anger and identify some of the possible repercussions if you continue with this practice. Then try bringing your anger, in all of its messiness, right to the throne of God. He knows you, he loves you, and he understands.

*Worship renews the
spirit as sleep
renews the body.*
—RICHARD CLARKE CABOT

NARRATIVE ON LIFE | A Changed Heart

Think of David and his relationship with Saul. Saul committed so much injustice against him, yet David refused to raise his hand against Saul because he was the Lord's anointed. Yet, in some of David's psalms, you can hear him saying, "I won't touch Saul, but Lord, if you want to deal with him, it would be fine with me."

Like David, we can take our wrath, anger, and vengeance to God. God says, "Bring it to me. I will help you walk through this." Then, at the footstool of God,

---

CREATIVE MESSAGE IDEA | Say It, Read It, Pray It, Sing It!

As you finish this message, consider doing one or more of the following things to help people focus on the God who is enthroned in power and glory:

Say it! Invite people to turn to the person next to them and say, "Our God reigns." Then have everyone say it together, as loud as they can!

Read it! Have everyone read selected verses of Psalm 96 in unison.

Pray it! Lead the congregation in a prayer expressing confidence and certainty that God is on the throne and that he is able to take care of his children.

Sing it! Close with a song expressing awareness and confidence that God rules and reigns.

Possible song ideas:

- "Bless His Holy Name," by Andrae Crouch
- "Come, Thou Almighty King," Author Unknown
- "Hosanna," by Carl Tuttle
- "How Excellent Is Your Name," by Michael W. Smith
- "Our God Is an Awesome God," by Rich Mullins
- "We Bow Down," by Twila Paris
- "What a Mighty God We Serve," Author Unknown
- "Be the Center," by Michael Frye
- "Shout to the North," by Martin Smith
- "Only a God Like You," by Tommy Walker

our anger and wrath begin to dissipate. Slowly, God changes our hearts. At the throne we discover that God can do what we can't. He can change our hearts. He can take a heart filled with anger and bitterness and begin to transform it. With his power, we can even learn to love our enemies.

SIGNIFICANT SCRIPTURE

Psalm 96

5. Enthronement Psalms

INTERPRETIVE INSIGHT | Enthronement Psalms

The final category of psalms we will learn about are enthronement psalms. These are psalms that recognize that this world may have troubles and that earthly leaders may not always be fair, but God is on the throne. These prayers turn our eyes upward, toward the very throne room of God, and remind us that no matter what we face, God is still enthroned.

NARRATIVE ON LIFE | Remember Who Is on the Throne

We need to learn from the example of God's people in the Old Testament. When times were hard, they kept their eyes on the one who rules and reigns. In the midst of sickness and in scarcity, when they were in exile, when they were under the oppression of the Assyrians or Babylonians, or when Jerusalem and the temple and all they loved was a distant memory, they would turn to these psalms. Every time they read Psalm 96 and other enthronement psalms, they remembered, "Our God reigns."

When we go through the trials this life brings, when we are hurting and feeling powerless, we need to look to the throne of God and remember that he rules. Also, when we talk with other Christ followers who have lost their focus, we might need to point them back to the throne and remind them who is in charge of this universe.

NEW TESTAMENT CONNECTION

Where Do You Look?

In the New Testament we find a similar example in the book of Hebrews. The author writes in Hebrews 12:1-3:

> Therefore, since we are surrounded by such a great cloud of witnesses, let us throw off everything that hinders and the sin that so easily entangles, and let us run with perseverance the race marked out for us. Let us fix our eyes on Jesus, the author and perfecter of our faith, who for the joy set before him endured the cross, scorning its shame, and sat down at the right hand of the throne of God. Consider him who endured such opposition from sinful men, so that you will not grow weary and lose heart.

As followers of Jesus, we need to keep our eyes fixed on Jesus. He is on the throne, and when we remember this, everything takes on a different tone. We see life through the eyes of eternity.

ON THE LIGHTER SIDE | A Psalm for April 15

As we have already seen, there are both psalms of praise and psalms of lament. Different ones were used on different occasions. Think, for a moment, what kind of psalm would you use on April 15, a praise or lament? (Give time for those gathered to respond.) The answer is obvious, a lament! People have always complained about government and, particularly, taxes! But the psalms acknowledge that no matter how bad human government might get, God is still on the throne.

Enter the Romance

SONG OF SONGS

The Heart of the
MESSAGE

When God created human beings, he made men and women. His perfect plan was a man and woman together in covenant love and community. In Eden, before the Fall, God said, "Be fruitful and multiply." It is clear that human romance and sexual intimacy were part of God's perfect plan. Even in Paradise, before sin entered in, God saw his creation of a man and woman in intimate relationship and declared it "Very good!"

The Song of Songs is a celebration of God's plan for romantic and sexual intimacy in the covenant of a marriage relationship. It is a bold reminder that God made us male and female and that his plan is still good. No matter how the world misuses God's good gifts, he always has the power and desire to restore them to his original plan.

The Heart of the
MESSENGER

Get ready to blush! Teaching from Song of Songs is a roller-coaster ride of passion, excitement, and intimacy. There is no way to teach this book with integrity and avoid the presence of honest expressions of romantic love and clear longings for sexual fulfillment. If you feel uncomfortable addressing these topics, it is time to pray for God's strength and leading. God celebrates the goodness of human romance, and so should we. If you are married but your relationship is not healthy and filled with romance, let this be a time to seek the Lord for a new flame to begin burning in your marriage.

Brief Message OUTLINE

1. Setting the Scene
2. Movement 1: Anticipation (1:1–3:5)
3. Movement 2: The Wedding and the Honeymoon (3:6–5:1)
4. Movement 3: Romance and Relationship (5:2–8:14)

1. Setting the Scene

NARRATIVE ON THE TEXT | ### An Allegory of the Church or a Love Story?

There are those who teach that the Song of Songs is really an allegory of God's love for the church. Generally people who hold this position have not read this book very closely. There is no indication of that anywhere in the text.

Song of Songs starts right in with kissing in the very first section and then it really gets going! It is a raw, unabashed, uninhibited celebration of romance and sexual attraction and passion between a man and a woman. Every indication, from looking at the text of this book, is that it is not an allegory about the church but an honest expression of love between two people.

NARRATIVE ON THE TEXT | ### Meeting the Characters

There are three main characters in the Song of Songs:

The woman: She is often called "the beloved." This woman is deeply in love and longs for her lover (the man). She is bold in her expressions of praise for the man's character. She also freely expresses her longing for intimacy and the depth of love she has for the man.

The man: He is called "the lover." This man is a common shepherd, but the woman sees him like a king. He is also bold in his declaration of love and is quick to praise his beloved. He celebrates her beauty and rejoices in her love.

The friends of the woman: They speak in concert together. Their combined voice celebrates the relationship of the man and woman and cheers them on in their relationship.

As you read the Song of Songs in most Bibles today, you will find captions that tell who is speaking. These headings are not in the Hebrew text. They have been supplied by interpreters to help us understand who is speaking at each point in the story. Because this is a poetic book, these title headings help us stay in touch with the drama and movement of the book.

NARRATIVE ON THE TEXT | ### Scenes in the Drama

There are three primary movements in the Song of Songs, which help us follow the plotline of the book. They are:

Movement 1: Anticipation (1:1–3:5). As you read this section, you meet a couple who is crazy in love. They can't wait to be together. They long for each other. But they are not married yet, so they dream, wait, and prepare for that day.

Movement 2: The wedding and honeymoon (3:6–5:1). This section is a poetic, highly stylized description of a wedding. It's a picture of commitment and covenant.

Movement 3: Their relationship after the wedding (romance and relationship) (5:2–8:14). The rest of the book is a celebration of love, romance, and the joy of covenantal sexual intimacy. It is a great reminder that true romantic fulfillment begins on the wedding day but does not end there.

NARRATIVE ON LIFE | **How to Hear This Message**

Some of those who are hearing this message are in marriages that are terrific. Others feel trapped in marriages that may be quite painful. There are also people who are married, but their spouse is not a believer. Almost every possible marital situation is represented in most churches.

No matter what your situation, God has something to say to you through the Song of Songs. Even those who are not married have a great deal to learn from this book. Every person who is gathered should be asking the question: "God, what do you have to say to me through this book of the Bible?" We must try to refrain from the temptation to think about what we wish someone else (even a spouse) would learn from these words. God wants us to ask, "God, what do you want to say *to me*?"

For those who are *married*, it is helpful to remember when your heart was the most tender toward your spouse. It may be when you first met and fell in love. Perhaps it was at your wedding, or else at some other point in your relationship. No matter when it was, even if it has been a long time since you have felt this way, try to remember what it felt like when your heart was tender toward your spouse.

Some of those gathered are *single*. Marriage may still be on the horizon. It could be something you are longing to experience. You can ask God, "What do you have to teach me about marriage and the kind of marriage that would honor you and bring joy?" Or, perhaps the question you need to ask is, "How could I support a married couple that I care about?"

ON THE LIGHTER SIDE | **What a Place to Start!**

The books of the Bible start in many different ways. Genesis begins with creation. Matthew starts with a record of the ancestral line of Jesus. Only Song of Songs begins with kissing! Just listen to the opening words of this book. Or better yet, read them together:

Let him kiss me with the kisses of his mouth—
for your love is more delightful than wine.

This book begins with the woman expressing her longing for the man to kiss her! No other book of the Bible opens with kissing (first base) and then goes on to hit a home run!

This is not Leviticus! It is a book unlike anything else in the Old or New Testament.

SIGNIFICANT SCRIPTURE

Song of Songs 1:1–3:5

Some of those gathered have *lost a spouse*. You were married and your spouse died. Maybe part of what God wants to do is to help you experience some moments of thankful remembering. God may engage you in a combination of both grief and comfort.

For those who have walked through the painful experience of *divorce*, it may be that God wants to remind them of the tenderness and love that can exist between a man and a woman. God made this relationship to be "good" and wants us to remember the beauty of his perfect plan, even if our experiences have not mirrored what God has in mind.

2. Movement 1: Anticipation

ILLUSTRATION | My Big Fat Greek Wedding

In the box office smash *My Big Fat Greek Wedding*, there is a scene where the mother takes her daughter aside and passes on an important piece of information. It is just before the wedding and the honeymoon. The mother lets her know that Greek women are not passive in the romance department. Her advice to her daughter is this: "Greek women might be lambs in the kitchen, but they are lions in the bedroom."

ON THE LIGHTER SIDE | Confession Time

To this day people are still fascinated with names. When a woman is going to be married, she will often practice writing her new name. Now it is confession time. By a showing of hands, how many of the women here spent time practicing writing their new name before you were married? Are there any men who want to admit that they practiced writing their wife's new name?

HISTORICAL CONTEXT | Your Name

In Song of Songs 1:3 the woman says, "Your name is like perfume." She's captivated by his name. This often happens with deep attraction. We can become fascinated by the name of a person we love.

But there is more happening here than just a mere fascination with a name. A name in the Scriptures generally refers to someone's *identity, reputation,* or *character.* This is why God's people were always careful to honor his name and never misuse it. God's name was equivalent to his character. Thus, when the woman is saying that her lover's name is like a pleasing fragrance, she is speaking of who he is as a person. She is deeply drawn to the character of this man. He is a man of deep integrity, honesty, and loyalty; he can be trusted.

INTERPRETIVE INSIGHT | ## The Need for Balance

Throughout the Bible we find many warnings, cautions, and safeguards concerning the potential dangers of human sexuality when it is expressed outside a covenant relationship between a man and a woman. The Bible has many examples of what happens when people mishandle sexuality. Those are all important, and they bring a much needed balance to our understanding of sexuality. We do not, however, find those warnings in the Song of Songs. This book is a celebration of the goodness of covenantal romance.

LIFE APPLICATION | ## A Word of Caution

This is a word for every young person and every single person—whatever age. Be careful about whom you give your heart to. Be sure to examine their character closely and thoroughly. Be sure their name has a fragrance like perfume and not manure. Some of the saddest stories you will ever hear involve people who develop a passionate attachment to somebody with an untrustworthy character. Get to know their name, their character, their reputation, before you make any lasting commitments.

LIFE APPLICATION | ## A Call to Celebrate

If you are married to someone with a good name, tell them how grateful you are. Let them know how much it means to you. Express the depth of your appreciation for their name in a letter, a poem, a song, a piece of art, in any way you can. Make sure you tell them how much it means to you that they are a person of character and integrity. Make a point of celebrating their name any chance you get. Also, freely tell others how much you appreciate the integrity and character of your spouse.

HISTORICAL CONTEXT

Beware . . . Song of Songs

Jewish parents in ancient days actually had an age restriction on the Song of Songs. Young boys were not to read this book until they were old enough. Some books of the Bible were rated G, but Song of Songs was rated R and was restricted until parents felt it was the right time for their children to read it.

HISTORICAL CONTEXT | ## Women in the Ancient World

Notice that the woman is the first to speak in the Song of Songs. She is honest, bold, and clear in what she is longing to have—kisses! We often think of women in the Middle East (especially the ancient Middle East) as being modest and even prudish. We think about the veils and long robes, and we can forget that they were women with the same desires and longing women have today. As we walk through this song, it becomes clear that the woman has a level of desire and passion every bit as powerful as the man has. It also becomes apparent that God is so pleased with her desires (and the man's longing) that he includes all of it in Scripture.

NARRATIVE ON THE TEXT | He Said, She Said

In the Song of Songs 1 we hear the man and woman speaking to each other. We need to realize that they use words and images that might seem strange to us, but their passion shows through. The woman speaks and declares her desire for her lover, she celebrates his name, and then she calls out for him. In 1:7 she says:

> Tell me, you whom I love, where you graze your flock
>> and where you rest your sheep at midday.
> Why should I be like a veiled woman
>> beside the flocks of your friends?

We find out a little bit more about the identity of the groom here. He is a common shepherd. He may not be wealthy, but he is like the king to her. Her words reveal that she longs to be with him.

Next, the man goes on to speak to her in these words (1:9):

> I liken you, my darling, to a mare
>> harnessed to one of the chariots of Pharaoh.

INTERPRETIVE INSIGHT | "The Delight Factor"

There is a striking feature that runs through this book. It might be called "the delight factor" in the conversation of a man and a woman who love each other. Behind their words is a deep desire to build each other up. They get creative in how they do this and in the words they use. Their words pour out of a generous heart. Each has a deep longing to build up the other and celebrate who they are.

ON THE LIGHTER SIDE | You Look Like a Horse!

Imagine a wife taking her husband to a mall to help her pick out a dress for a wedding they will be attending. She gathers a few options and heads into the dressing room. He sits in the special "husband-chair," strategically positioned just outside of the dressing room area. There he waits for the moment she reappears. He knows what the question will be, for he has sat in this chair before.

"How do I look?"

He pauses, reflects, and then he says, *You look like a horse!*

Let's be honest, this would not go over very well! In our day, calling a woman a horse is not a complimentary thing. Even if he clarified by saying she looked like she was harnessed to a chariot, this would not help. Some images just don't transfer over from the Song of Songs to the Nordstrom's changing room.

In those days, Pharaoh's horses were prized above all others. The woman would have taken these words as a flattering compliment. All through this book we need to realize that the images that seem strange to us were understood in a positive light.

LIFE APPLICATION | A Time to Praise

Husbands and wives today need to learn to praise the good they see in each other. Maybe we need to discover the dove-like beauty that is in the eyes of our spouse. If we have not looked deeply into our spouse's eyes in a long time, it is time to start gazing.

A loving husband should find things about his wife that he celebrates and tell her on a regular basis. In turn, his wife should receive these words of celebration. She should not say, "No. It's not true. I'm not that pretty." She needs to receive his words of praise and drink in his love.

In the same way, a wife should compliment and affirm the good attributes she sees in her husband. When she sees something in his appearance or character that is praiseworthy, she should let him know. He also needs to learn to receive her words of blessing.

NARRATIVE ON THE TEXT | Playful Interactions

There's a playful aspect to the banter that's going on with the woman and the man. She is saying that she feels ordinary and plain, but she is also giving him an opportunity to say that he sees her in a different light. When it's overdone, it can be manipulative, like fishing for compliments. But when it is honest, it can open the door for mutual expressions of blessing and affirmation.

This can be a playful way of saying, "I'm open to your expressions of love. I really am. I'll receive them. I'm interested." The lover responds by saying: "Like a lily among thorns"—because every other woman in the world is a thorn, it causes pain even to look at them compared to you—"is my darling among the young women."

HISTORICAL CONTEXT | A Rose and a Lily

In Song of Songs 2:1 the woman says, "I am a rose of Sharon, a lily of the valleys." That sounds a little boastful at first. "I'm a rose, I'm a lily—look at me!" But Old Testament scholars say that a rose in ancient times was not like what we think of in our day. It was not something you would get from a florist's shop. It was a common, not a valuable flower. It was a type of crocus and was not noted for its beauty or expense.

When the woman calls herself a "lily of the valley," she is speaking of a plain, everyday blossom. It was the kind of flower that would be picked up, smelled, and then tossed aside by any shepherd. In reality, these are modest words. She is saying, "I'm not that attractive. I'm just kind of average."

NARRATIVE ON LIFE | A Culture of Two

Throughout the Song of Songs both the man and woman use pet names for the other. The man uses the name "my darling" nine times in the book. The woman also has her pet names for the man. This practice is still common today. One contemporary psychologist notes that strong marriage relationships actually create what he calls a "culture of two."

This is expressed by things like special nicknames. He notes that the nicknames couples have for each other tend to come from one of three categories: food, animals, and body parts. Some examples are: sugar, honey, teddy bear, and that kind of thing. Sometimes we combine them and come up with real creative options like: sugar lips, honey bear, muffin ears, and other combinations.

ILLUSTRATION | The Most Tender Language

Some people even create a private love language that seems almost like baby talk. They would be embarrassed if others heard the way they communicate with each other in intimate moments. C. S. Lewis writes about this in a book called *The Four Loves*. He makes note of a certain scientist who discovered that certain animals (including specific species of birds) do a similar thing. They make infantile sounds normally made only by young birds of their species when courting another bird. Lewis says the reason for this is that it is the most tender language. Among animals and people, it expresses a tender heart.

LIFE APPLICATION | A Generous Heart

Here's a question for those who are married: Do you relate to your spouse with a generous heart or a stingy heart? Do you give sincere, authentic praise? Do you speak words that honor and value your spouse? Do you treasure secrets together—things that only the two of you hold and share? Do you build rituals into your lives? Do you go on dates with each other? Do you create memories? Do you guard your culture of two?

NARRATIVE ON THE TEXT | Belong to Each Other

There is a classic phrase from the Song of Songs in 2:16. The woman says, "My lover is mine and I am his." This is such an important declaration that it gets repeated almost verbatim in 6:3 and again in 7:10. To this day it is often used by Jewish brides at weddings. It's a statement of possession: We belong to each other. This is not an unhealthy, controlling, or jealous sense of belonging. Rather, this is an expression of the deep meaning of covenant.

ON THE LIGHTER SIDE

Just Kidding!

Some people use baby talk when they relate to their dogs. Most of us have heard this. C. S. Lewis says this is really stupid. No, he didn't actually say that. Just kidding!

Through the Old Testament we learn that God is deeply concerned about covenants. God's covenant is, "I will be your God, and you will be my people." In a similar way, the marital covenant is, "My lover is mine and I am his." When these words are promised between two human beings in marriage, they are saying, "There's not much you can count on in this world. Your health may go south, your pension fund may collapse, your career may never look like what you hoped it would look like, and your appearance may change over the years, but you can count on one thing: As long as this heart is beating, it's yours. I will not give my heart and body to anybody else in the way that I give it to you."

LIFE APPLICATION | **I'm Not Going Anywhere**

Sometimes when a relationship is going through hard times, the best you can say is, "I'm not going anywhere." In a world where everything seems dispensable, we need to commit that our covenants mean something. When times are hard and we feel like giving up, we remember the promise we made to our spouse and God and we declare, "No matter how hard things get, I will never even entertain the idea of giving up. We are in this marriage together and with God's help, we will make it!"

3. Movement 2: The Wedding and the Honeymoon

NARRATIVE ON THE TEXT | **A Wedding Scene**

The next section in Song of Songs begins in 3:6. The anticipation is over, and the wedding day has come. There are disagreements among scholars about how to interpret this scene. Some people think Solomon is the literal bridegroom being described. This is unlikely for at least two reasons: (1) This man is a shepherd (1:7) while Solomon was not. (2) The major theme of this book is the mutual exclusiveness of the man and the woman ("My lover is mine and I am his"), while Solomon had seven hundred wives and three hundred concubines. He was not a model of exclusive love.

It is likely that "Solomon" in 3:7, 9, and 11 is kind of a code name for the groom. Poetry often works that way. The pageantry and the court imagery used here expresses something important. When the woman looks at this man, he may be just a shepherd, but in the eyes of the one who loves him, he's a king.

CREATIVE MESSAGE IDEA

A Blessed Arrangement

You may want to use the brief wedding scene from the movie *The Princess Bride*. (Be sure to get permission.)

SIGNIFICANT SCRIPTURE

Song of Songs 3:6–5:1

LIFE APPLICATION | How Do You See People?

In God's eyes, the world is not divided up into important people like Solomon and CEOs, and then unimportant people like shepherds. In God's eyes, everybody bears his image. In God's eyes, everybody is made to reign with him. True love enables us to see just a little bit of what God sees when he looks at us through the eyes of Christ. When we love somebody, we can see the ragged shepherd, but we can also see a king or queen.

So many people in our world are good at seeing faults. Those who are married are always tempted to focus on the shortcomings of their spouses. What we need to learn to see, in all of our relationships, are the good qualities. We need to learn to see people as God does. If you tend to be quick to judge and find yourself seeing the weaknesses in everyone you meet, it may be time to ask God to give you new eyes.

HISTORICAL CONTEXT | Understanding the Images

Look at Song of Songs 4:1–5. Again, the man is praising his beloved's beauty. Notice the various images he uses (some are highlighted below):

How beautiful you are, my darling!
Oh, how beautiful!
    Your eyes behind your veil are *doves.*
Your hair is like a *flock of goats*
    descending from Mount Gilead.
Your teeth are like a *flock of sheep just shorn,*
    coming up from the washing.
Each has its twin;
    not one of them is alone.
Your lips are like a scarlet ribbon;
    your mouth is lovely.
Your temples behind your veil
    are like the halves of a
        pomegranate.
Your neck is like the *tower of David,*
    built with elegance;
on it hang a thousand shields,
    all of them shields of warriors.
Your two breasts are like two fawns,
    like twin fawns of a gazelle
        that browse among the lilies.

This is the kind of imagery that tends to bog some people down when they read through the Song of Songs. Here are some quick insights that may help make sense of this imagery.

"Your eyes . . . are doves." Doves in that culture were prized, especially for their color. In the sun, they were kind of a translucent gray. This is the man's way of saying he sees her eyes and they are beautiful.

When you look into somebody's eyes, it's a very intimate thing. It is a soul gaze. Their eyes will tell you if they're happy, if they're sad, or if they're beaten down by life. If you are deeply attached to someone, you know the color of their eyes because you have looked into them many times. This man has looked deeply into this pair of eyes.

"Your hair is like a flock of goats." This is not a common compliment in our day, but in biblical culture it made sense. When a large herd of goats came down a hill, they would wind around it in a way that looked quite striking and attractive from a distance. This was the lover's way

of saying, "Your hair is thick and wavy. I like how it curls. It looks wonderful."

"Your temples . . . are like the halves of a pomegranate." The idea here is that her head is symmetrical. Today we talk about somebody having good bone structure. He is appreciating the shape and size of her head.

"Your neck is like the tower of David." The neck was a symbol of strength. Even in our day we have a similar phrase: "Her head will not be easily turned by someone who comes along." This is about elegant strength. Also, the tower of David was covered with shields that shone in the sun. He is admiring her neck for its beauty.

This is an ecstatic celebration of the worth of the one the man loves. He is using images that would be deeply compelling to the Middle Eastern heart. He's going on record to say, "This is how much I want you. This is how deeply I love you. This is how firmly I devote myself to you. I notice your beauty, and I have to express it!"

NARRATIVE ON THE TEXT | The Wedding Unfolds

Now the groom speaks. His anticipation has mounted to this point, and their wedding day has come (4:9–11):

> You have stolen my heart, my sister, my bride;
>   you have stolen my heart
> with one glance of your eyes,
>   with one jewel of your necklace.
> How delightful is your love, my sister, my bride!
>   How much more pleasing is your love than wine,
>   and the fragrance of your perfume than any spice!
> Your lips drop sweetness as the honeycomb, my bride;
>   milk and honey are under your tongue.
>   The fragrance of your garments is like that of Lebanon.

Notice that in this section the title "bride" is used for the first time. Most likely the use of this word here is to be understood as the place in the wedding where the man is making his vows.

LIFE APPLICATION | Remember Your Vows

If you are married, take out a copy of your wedding vows and read through them together. How are you doing at keeping this covenant? How can you be more faithful to live out the promises you made on that important day? You may even want to have a copy of your wedding vows framed and place it somewhere you will see it on a regular basis.

NARRATIVE ON THE TEXT | The Honeymoon

Right in the context of the wedding and the honeymoon, we read some intimate words (4:16–5:1). Notice that each of the three primary parties in this drama speaks:

ON THE LIGHTER SIDE | A Bad Tooth Millennium

"Your teeth are like a flock of sheep just shorn, coming up from the washing. Each has its twin." Let's be honest, that just sounds bizarre! But in those days it made sense—it really did. Remember, those were days when there were no dentists, orthodontists, toothpaste, toothbrushes, braces, fluoride in the water supply, or flossing. It was a bad millennium for teeth. Everybody had missing teeth. But, the beloved's teeth are lovely.

They are white. They look like sheep that have just been shorn and washed.

When the lover says that each of her teeth has a twin, it is his way of affirming the fact that she is not missing any teeth. There was a lower tooth for every upper tooth. He is noting that it is more attractive than if she had a few teeth missing.

The Beloved (the bride)
Awake, north wind,
　　and come, south wind!
Blow on my garden,
　　that its fragrance may spread abroad.
Let my lover come into his garden
　　and taste its choice fruits.

The Lover (the groom)
I have come into my garden, my sister, my bride;
　　I have gathered my myrrh with my spice.
I have eaten my honeycomb and my honey;
　　I have drunk my wine and my milk.

The Friends
Eat, O friends, and drink;
　　drink your fill, O lovers.

Again we see many word pictures intended to communicate what is happening here. It is not hard to decipher what these images mean. This is their wedding night. They are to enjoy the fullness and wonder of sexual expression within a covenantal relationship.

When the man and woman speak of a garden, they are not talking about a literal garden with sunflowers and rutabagas. This is a metaphorical way of saying, "Whew! Whee!" They are rejoicing in the intimacy God has given them. It is important to recognize that the man, the woman, and the friends all see the romantic and sexual expression of a married couple as something to be celebrated. The fact that this is all recorded in Scripture teaches us that God rejoices in this also.

HISTORICAL CONTEXT | **"My Sister, My Bride"**

The groom uses the phrase "my sister, my bride" a number of times in this book. This may seem strange to us, but in that culture family ties were the most binding ties of all. Blood was definitely thicker than water. He is saying, "My tie to you will be the most binding of all. All of the loyalties that would go into any relationship with a member of my birth family, I now give to you." When he calls her his sister, it is a high compliment and a sign of deep devotion.

LIFE APPLICATION | The Role of Friends

The friends in this scene are giving a toast to the bride and groom and cheering for their intimacy and closeness. There is a specific role that the friends play in this book of the Bible. They cheer, bless, and give positive direction to the couple. This is still the role of those who have friends who are married.

Marriages don't occur in vacuums. When we think about friends who are married, we should ask the question, "Is their marriage stronger and better because of me?" We can all learn more about how we can encourage and bless those who are married.

Praying faithfully for married couples is a great place to start. God also invites us to cheer and affirm when a marriage is strong and heading in the right direction. We can encourage our married friends, listen to them, and respond in ways that build hope. If a marriage is in trouble, we can encourage our friends to talk with a pastor or see a good Christian counselor. When a marriage is doing well, we can make specific observations about the good parts of the relationship we see and rejoice with our friends. Every marriage needs a cheering section, and it is an honor when we can be part of a chorus of voices that celebrate a good marriage.

4. Movement 3: Romance and Relationship

NARRATIVE ON THE TEXT | The Story Goes On

The wedding day is not the end; it is the beginning. Too many couples focus on the wedding day and the honeymoon and spend all of their time getting ready for this one short period of time. They forget that the marriage will last a lifetime. Song of Songs does not miss this reality. The rest of the book deals with the need to build a relationship and maintain a romantic and growing life of intimacy in marriage.

When we come to 5:2, we discover that the wedding and the honeymoon are over. We don't know how much time has passed, but the couple is now into their married life. This is kind of a dream sequence. The wife says, "I slept but my heart was awake" (5:2). The husband comes home from work. He has been out in the fields tending the sheep and is covered with dew. He has something specific on his mind.

As he comes to the door, you can almost hear him say, "I had to work late, dear. My head is covered with dew, but I'm home now." Then notice all of the pet names he throws in: "my sister, my darling, my dove, my flawless one." Can you guess what he has in mind?

PAUSE FOR PRAYER

Lifting Up Marriages

Take time as a group to pray for marriages. As a leader you might want to give some brief words to prompt those gathered as they pray:

- Pray for healing and restoration in marriages that are strained.
- Cry out to God on behalf of those who are widows and widowers. Pray for the comfort and strength of God to fill their hearts.
- Lift up words of thanksgiving for marriages that are strong and healthy.

SIGNIFICANT SCRIPTURE

Song of Songs 5:2–8:14

Her response is found in verse 3, "I have taken off my robe—must I put it on again? I have washed my feet—must I soil them again?" In other words, "Do I have to get up and let you in?" This is a Middle Eastern way of saying, "Not tonight, I've got a headache." Even in the Song of Songs marriage is not idealized to the point of being unrealistic.

NARRATIVE ON LIFE | Tough Times Will Come

Even in the strongest, most passionate marriages there will be tough times. Every couple needs to be ready for this. If you get married expecting perfect harmony, endless romance, and no conflict, you will be disappointed. The issue is not if we will face difficult days, it is how we will respond when these times come. These are the days when we need to receive God's power and grace when ours is in short supply. These are the times we need our chorus of friends to support and encourage us. These are the moments that we might need to seek the help of a professional Christian counselor to help us get perspective and tools that will help us move forward and build a marriage that honors God and brings blessing to our hearts.

LIFE APPLICATION | Unquenchable Love

As Song of Songs continues, there are more expressions of joy, celebrations of beauty, and expressions of commitment to make this relationship last. Then we come to one of the most beautiful sections of the entire book (8:6–7):

> Place me like a seal over your heart,
>   like a seal on your arm;
> for love is as strong as death,
>   its jealousy unyielding as the grave.
> It burns like blazing fire,
>   like a mighty flame.
> Many waters cannot quench love;
>   rivers cannot wash it away.
> If one were to give
>   all the wealth of his house for love,
>   it would be utterly scorned.

There is a closing declaration that their love will be unquenchable. In a world where intimacy, romance, and relationships seem to get snuffed out by busyness, apathy, unresolved conflict, financial stresses, poor communication, and selfishness, we need to hear these words. Love seems to get quenched each day, but it does not have to. If you are married, let this be the moment you say that your love will not be quenched. Commit to sit with your spouse and talk about how you can fan the flames of your marriage. What will it take to rekindle the spark of romance? What habits need to start? What needs to end? Who will keep you accountable to build a healthy relationship? How will you celebrate when you take steps forward on this journey?

CREATIVE MESSAGE IDEA

A Closing Song and Prayer

Have someone sing a closing song that is often used in weddings. Let these words strike a chord in the hearts of those who are married. Then, close with a prayer for God's power and blessing to be released in the marriages of those gathered.

CREATIVE MESSAGE IDEA | Live/Video Testimony

If you have a couple who has worked through a time of struggle but are now deeply committed to their marriage and growing in a very healthy direction, you may want to have them share a brief testimony at this time.

Solomon: Extreme Wisdom

1 KINGS 3:7-28; PROVERBS

The Heart of the
MESSAGE

God desires for us to walk and live in his wisdom. Although we may see wisdom as the ability to answer trivia questions or do well on tests, God sees it differently. Wisdom is the ability to make right decisions that honor him and move us toward his purposes for life. In this message each person will be challenged to find a proverb that they can carry in their heart in a way that will transform their lives. This message is about growing to understand and love God's wisdom so much that we long to see it grow in our lives.

The Heart of the
MESSENGER

As you prepare to bring this message, be sure to adopt a proverb from the six key verses in this message. Once you have chosen your proverb, commit it to memory. Spend a week meditating on this verse and let God's wisdom sink deeply into your heart. Ask God to shape your thoughts and actions around the message of this proverb. As you begin to see a transformed life, you will know that you are growing in wisdom.

Brief Message
OUTLINE

1. Meeting Solomon
2. Understanding Proverbs
3. Adopting a Proverb

1. Meeting Solomon

NARRATIVE ON LIFE | Important Questions

This may seem like a harsh question to ask at the beginning of a message, but it is an important one. Ask those gathered: "Have you ever done anything really stupid?"

The truth is that we have all done more stupid things than we want to remember. When we identify the reality of our poor decisions, we become profoundly aware of our need for God's wisdom.

Here are a couple of other questions that might be helpful for us to answer:

- Do you do stupid (unwise) things that you end up regretting on a fairly regular basis?

- Would you like for it to stop, or would you like to cut down on the number of stupid things you do?

The book of Proverbs was given by God to help us do exactly that: It teaches us to do less stupid things and to grow in our ability to live wisely.

SIGNIFICANT SCRIPTURE

1 Kings 3:7-28

NARRATIVE ON THE TEXT | Encounter with Solomon

At the beginning of 1 Kings, David is dying. This leads to a lot of intrigue and jockeying for the throne. The first few chapters describe a political mess, but God is still at work.

In chapter 3 God comes to Solomon in a dream. God says to him, "Ask me for whatever you want—anything." This is an interesting test. If God were to offer you or me anything in the world, we have to wonder what we would ask for. Solomon's response is amazing! He prays:

> "Now, O LORD my God, you have made your servant king in place of my father David. But I am only a little child and do not know how to carry out my duties. Your servant is here among the people you have chosen, a great people, too numerous to count or number. So *give your servant a discerning heart to govern your people and to distinguish between right and wrong*. For who is able to govern this great people of yours?" (1 Kings 3:7–9)

The text goes on to say God is pleased that Solomon asks for wisdom, for it shows that he is viewing himself as a servant. He could have asked for anything for himself, but he asks for a gift that will benefit the people that he is called to serve.

LIFE APPLICATION | Am I Passionate About Serving?

As we look at Solomon's desire to serve the people and as we are reminded of Jesus' example of service (and call for us to serve), we should take time to evaluate how much we serve. Do we tend to like people waiting on us and serving us more than us serving them? Is the natural disposition of our heart to serve others? Have we found practical ways to serve in our home, on our campus, at our workplace, and in the church? God calls us to a posture of service, and we need to learn that the wise person follows this call.

ILLUSTRATION | Amazing Wisdom

Right after Solomon's prayer, we read a famous story that shows how his wisdom is put to the test in a dramatic way. Two prostitutes come before Solomon. One of their sons has died in the night. Both claim that the living boy is theirs.

"Bring me a sword," Solomon says. "We'll just cut the remaining baby in half and you can each have a portion." Then the real mother reveals herself. Rather than have her son killed, she is willing to give him up. Solomon identifies this woman as the true mother and returns her son to her arms.

What a powerful picture of wisdom in action!

INTERPRETIVE INSIGHT | Justice for All

In the story of the two women and their babies there is mention of their occupation. Did you notice what it was? They were prostitutes. In the ancient world prostitutes were generally slaves because they had been sold by their own parents at a very young age. In that culture they were despised. They were the lowest of the low. In those days people with wealth could get a hearing and justice, but often the poor and outcasts were not able to get justice. The writer is showing us that Solomon is committed to making sure *everybody* in the kingdom receives justice, even the outcast and marginalized.

NEW TESTAMENT CONNECTION

The Ultimate Servant

In the gospel of Mark we hear Jesus declare why he came to this earth. When we know who he was, this is astounding. Jesus said, "For even the Son of Man did not come to be served, but to serve, and to give his life as a ransom for many" (Mark 10:45). In John 13:1–17, Jesus washes the feet of his disciples, an act of incredible service. And in all four of the Gospels, we watch as Jesus extends the ultimate act of service by laying down his life to pay for our sins. His example is one that should be duplicated in the lives of all who are his followers.

HISTORICAL CONTEXT | Good Times

In 1 Kings 4:20 we get a picture of life at the beginning of Solomon's reign. We read that "Judah and Israel were as numerous as the sand on the seashore; they ate, they drank and they were happy." What a pleasant description of life. This was a good time.

Solomon was sovereign over all the kingdoms from the Euphrates River to the land of the Philistines and all the way down to the border of Egypt. People brought tribute and gifts to him from all over the known world. We go on to read of the vast wealth of Solomon and how peace prevailed and the kingdom expanded. From an external perspective, Solomon had military success, economic prosperity, peace in the land, and everything the people ever dreamed and hoped for. These verses show us the highest point Israel will ever achieve. For Israel this is their one, brief, shining moment as a people. It was a golden era in the history of Israel.

NEW TESTAMENT
CONNECTION

Who Could Be Greater than Solomon?

Solomon led the people to a time of unparalleled prosperity, peace, and hope. Yet one day there would come a leader even greater than Solomon. In Matthew 12:42 Jesus makes a remarkable statement about himself: "Now one greater than Solomon is here." We tend to skim over those words, but to the listeners in Jesus' day this bold statement would put them on tilt. In their minds Solomon was one of the greatest and most glorious people in their history. How could an obscure, impoverished, and homeless carpenter's son says he is greater than Solomon?

Jesus is declaring that God's kingdom was never really about land, armies, wealth, and power. It was always intended to be a kingdom of changed hearts. This was a great message in Jesus' day, when the people of Israel were still looking for a military and economic kingdom. It is also an important reminder in our day because we can fall into the trap of believing that God's ultimate plan is economic and political power for his people. But there is so much more to God's kingdom.

NARRATIVE ON THE TEXT | How Wise Was This Guy?

First Kings 4:29–34 gives us this description of Solomon:

> God gave Solomon wisdom and very great insight, and a breadth of understanding as measureless as the sand on the seashore. Solomon's wisdom was greater than the wisdom of all the men of the East, and greater than all the wisdom of Egypt. He was wiser than any other man, including Ethan the Ezrahite—wiser than Heman, Calcol and Darda, the sons of Mahol. And his fame spread to all the surrounding nations. He spoke three thousand proverbs and his songs numbered a thousand and five. He described plant life, from the cedar of Lebanon to the hyssop that grows out of walls. He also taught about animals and birds, reptiles and fish. Men of all nations came to listen to Solomon's wisdom, sent by all the kings of the world, who had heard of his wisdom.

It was a tradition in the ancient Near East to have wise men who dispensed wisdom. Kings were also expected to be wise and to surround themselves with counselors who understood wisdom.

ILLUSTRATION | The Best of the Best

If you follow distance running at all, you know that Africa produces many of the best long-distance runners in the world. If you plan to win a marathon or an Olympic event in distance running, you had better be ready to compete against some great runners from Kenya. You can count on it!

In the same way, in Solomon's day the people of the Near East were the long-distance runners when it came to wisdom. They were famed. They were legendary. Yet we are told that the wisdom of Solomon lapped them all!

CREATIVE MESSAGE IDEA | Map Time

Look at a map that shows the breadth and expanse of the kingdom under Solomon. You may also want to remind people that in Solomon's day, the people were realizing the promise made to Abraham so many years before. Their descendants were as numerous as the sands of the seashore and were safe in the land of Canaan.

INTERPRETIVE INSIGHT | All People Are Welcome!

At the dedication of the temple Solomon prays one of the greatest prayers in all Scripture. Here is a part of his prayer:

> "As for the foreigner who does not belong to your people Israel but has come from a distant land because of your name— for men will hear of your great name and your mighty hand and your outstretched arm—when he comes and prays toward this temple, then hear from heaven, your dwelling place, and do whatever the foreigner asks of you, so that all the peoples of the earth may know your name and fear you, as do your own people Israel, and may know that this house I have built bears your Name." (1 Kings 8:41–43)

God said to Abraham many centuries earlier, "And all peoples on earth will be blessed through you" (Genesis 12:3). Even in the Old Testament, Israel was never chosen just for their own sake, but for the sake of the world. God's heart has always been to bless the whole earth and all people, never just one group.

INTERPRETIVE INSIGHT | Solomon's Greatest Legacy

What was Solomon's greatest legacy and contribution to God's people? Certainly he brought a time of unparalleled fame and prosperity. His building of the temple ranks near the top of the list. He expanded the borders of Israel. All of these things are noteworthy. But they are not his greatest legacy.

The proverbs are Solomon's greatest contribution to the people of God. All through his life Solomon reminded the people that wisdom is a path they must walk every day. More important than Solomon's building projects, expansion of the kingdom, or the time of peace he ushered in is the book of Proverbs and the wisdom that continues to speak to each new generation.

NEW TESTAMENT CONNECTION
God's Call to Us

Jesus reinforced what God taught his people through Abraham, Solomon, and so many others in the Old Testament. Even though the Old Testament is filled with clear calls for God's people to reach out to those who were not a part of them, many still missed it. This is why Jesus was so emphatic about this. Some of the last words Jesus spoke reinforce this calling:

> Then Jesus came to them and said, "All authority in heaven and on earth has been given to me. Therefore go and make disciples of all nations, baptizing them in the name of the Father and of the Son and of the Holy Spirit, and teaching them to obey everything I have commanded you. And surely I am with you always, to the very end of the age." (Matthew 28:18–20)

> But you will receive power when the Holy Spirit comes on you; and you will be my witnesses in Jerusalem, and in all Judea and Samaria, and to the ends of the earth. (Acts 1:8)

HISTORICAL CONTEXT | The Importance of the Temple

One of the high points of Solomon's reign was the building of God's temple. This achievement meant more to Israel than almost anything else. Solomon spent seven years and countless amounts of wealth on this project. That temple is described in great detail (much like the tabernacle was) because it was extremely important to the Israelites. The temple was supposed to be a glorified, permanent tabernacle to house the ark of the covenant. This became the central place of worship for God's people.

HISTORICAL CONTEXT

A Curriculum for Wisdom

The proverbs Solomon wrote were collected, most likely, as a part of an effort to train and develop a whole new generation of leaders that would serve under Solomon. The purpose of this book was to impart wisdom to all who were willing to receive it. It is likely that the book of Proverbs was gathered into a formal collection so that it could be used in the tutoring and developing of leaders for Israel.

2. Understanding Proverbs

INTERPRETIVE INSIGHT | Wisdom Defined

In the Old Testament, wisdom is fundamentally the ability to make right decisions. In ancient times, wisdom was not primarily about how high your IQ was or how educated you were. It was not primarily about information. In our day, we tend to confuse information with wisdom. Do you ever feel overloaded with information? That's not wisdom. Wisdom is practical. It is the ability to discern what the noble, constructive, God-honoring course of action will be in actual, real-life situations. And then, wisdom is making the choice to do it! That's wisdom.

A fool, on the other hand, is not primarily an ignorant person—not primarily someone with a low IQ. Folly in the Old Testament is a problem of the will, not the mind. At its heart, folly is rebellion against God, moral depravity, spiritual blindness, and social irresponsibility toward others. A fool may know all the answers, but his problem is that he cannot seem to do the wise thing.

NARRATIVE ON LIFE | Proverbs—A Life Saver

Proverbs is an urgently important book for followers of Christ today. It is not just a casual collection of affirmations that we can take or leave as we see fit. It has been written and given to us to save us from folly, which leads to death. The stakes are high when it comes to this book. If we read it, understand it, and live it out, we are on the path to life. If we ignore Proverbs, we do so at our own peril!

CREATIVE MESSAGE IDEA | Who and Why?

Take time to read the first seven verses of Proverbs. These verses hold the key to who this book was written for and why it was written. Ask everyone who has their own Bible to circle each person this book is written for and then to underline any clues as to why it was written.

The proverbs of Solomon son of David, king of Israel:
for attaining wisdom and discipline;
    for understanding words of insight;
for acquiring a disciplined and prudent life,
    doing what is right and just and fair;

for giving prudence to the simple,
    knowledge and discretion to the young—
let the wise listen and add to their learning,
    and let the discerning get guidance—
for understanding proverbs and parables,
    the sayings and riddles of the wise.
The fear of the LORD is the beginning of knowledge,
    but fools despise wisdom and discipline.

ILLUSTRATION | A Gold Ring in a Pig's Snout

Proverbs were deliberately written to be catchy. They were often visual. Sometimes there was even a comic visual element to the proverbs. Try Proverbs 11:22 on for size:

> Like a gold ring in a pig's snout
>> is a beautiful woman who shows no discretion.

What a memorable mental image. What a great warning for people who might get married one day. You can almost hear Proverbs crying out: "If you get hooked up with somebody who has poor judgment and a defective character just because they're physically attractive—beware! If you value looks over integrity, you are not the brightest bulb on the chandelier."

INTERPRETIVE INSIGHT | A Classic Example

A classic example of a proverb that some people try to make a law is Proverbs 22:6: "Train a child in the way he should go, and when he is old he will not turn from it." This proverb was never intended to be taken as an ironclad guarantee, but many people try to read it this way.

This proverb does not guarantee that if you raise a little girl in the church, teach her the Bible, and do your best, you can be assured that she will become a devoted follower of Jesus. It also doesn't mean that if your children go down a destructive or rebellious path that you did a bad job and didn't train them right. Adam and Eve went down the wrong path, but that doesn't mean God (their heavenly Father) did something wrong.

ON THE LIGHTER SIDE | Writing a Proverb

Writing an effective proverb takes a brilliant mind. A good proverb has to be brief and pithy, have deep insight into human nature, and get expressed in a few unforgettable words that you just cannot get out of your brain. They stick with you. Every culture produces a few minds capable of this kind of writing. In our day, many of them live in Nashville and write country and western music.

Here are a few titles of country and western songs that are proverb-like in their brevity and brilliance.

"How Can I Miss You If You Won't Go Away?"
"I've Got You on My Conscience, but at Least You're off My Back"
"I Would Have Wrote You a Letter, But I Couldn't Spell . . . Yuck!"
"I Bought the Shoes That Just Walked Out on Me"

These are all short, sweet, to the point, and certainly memorable. That's the way a proverb works.

Proverbs 22:6 is simply wisdom for parents. Our children grow up, to a large extent, as we shape them, for better or for worse. They are likely to go in the direction and pursue the trajectory that we trained them for. So, if we train up a son or daughter to know and love Jesus, there is a good chance they will. But this is not a guarantee.

NARRATIVE ON THE TEXT | Read Slowly and Reflect Deeply

Another important feature of Proverbs is they are designed to force us to think about them slowly and ponder them over time. It does not benefit us to skim this book. Proverbs may not make sense right away, but a day, week, or month after we have read them, as we ponder their meaning, we just may have a moment of enlightenment. All of a sudden we stop and say, "I get it!" The meaning unfolds over time. Then, when it makes sense, we begin the process of letting its wisdom shape our lives.

Here is a great example from Proverbs 24:27:

> Finish your outdoor work
> and get your fields ready;
> after that, build your house.

What does this mean? Does it mean that if a husband doesn't mow the grass, he is supposed to sleep in a tent? Is that the idea? Well, in that culture outdoor work (farming) was income-producing. It was the primary way of making a living and providing for a family. Building a house was income-draining. This proverb is telling us, "It is unwise to spend money you don't have." If we were going to write this proverb in our day it might be, "Get a job before you get a Jaguar."

HISTORICAL CONTEXT | Understanding the Type of Literature You Are Reading

If we are going to benefit from Proverbs, it is crucial that we understand the kind of teaching Proverbs is meant to give us. If we don't get this right, we will become frustrated along the way. It is important that we clarify the nature of a proverb, as we have other kinds of literature in the Old Testament. A proverb is a specific genre and must be read in light of this.

Three specific kinds of literature in the Old Testament are as follows:

Laws: A law is a command you must always obey.
Promises: A promise is a guarantee that is always true.
Proverbs: A proverb is a catchy observation about the way things generally are.

Proverbs are designed to give helpful guidance in real-life situations. But they are not absolutes, nor are they promises.

NARRATIVE ON THE TEXT | Take Care

The biblical proverbs themselves warn to take care with how we handle and use them. Proverbs 26:9 says, "Like a thornbush in a drunkard's hand is a proverb in the mouth of a fool." Just think about what happens when an inebriated, unsteady person grabs a plant full of thorns. Such a person is going to get hurt. The same thing happens when a fool starts using a proverb. He is going to get hurt. She is going to misuse it. And others may get hurt as well.

The book of Proverbs invites us to take care and use discernment. The Israelites devoted themselves to this, and so should we. They studied, meditated on, practiced, and committed the Proverbs to memory. They celebrated these proverbs because they found the proverbs changed their lives.

> *Nothing is foolproof in the hands of a fool.*
> —BENJAMIN FRANKLIN

NARRATIVE ON LIFE | We Can't Seem to Stop

Ask a gambler: "Do you think your chronic gambling is a good, long-term bet to produce a worthwhile life?" There is no doubt that this person will say, "No!"

Ask a hot-tempered person: "Is your strategy of bursting out in anger helping you pursue the kind of relational intimacy you most long for?" They will tell you it does not.

CREATIVE MESSAGE IDEA | Laws, Promises, and Proverbs

Read specific passages (listed below) and project them on a screen if you can. Then ask everyone present to whisper to the person next to them if it is a law, promise, or proverb.

· *Example 1:* "Love the LORD your God with all your heart and with all your soul and with all your strength." (Deuteronomy 6:5)

This is a law. There are never any exceptions. We are always to love God with all we are and have.

· *Example 2:* "No, in all these things we are more than conquerors through him who loved us. For I am convinced that neither death nor life, neither angels nor demons, neither the present nor the future, nor any powers, neither height nor depth, nor anything else in all creation, will be able to separate us from the love of God that is in Christ Jesus our Lord." (Romans 8:37–39)

This is a promise. Again, there are no exceptions. Nothing can separate us from God's love.

· *Example 3:* "Lazy hands make a man poor, but diligent hands bring wealth." (Proverbs 10:4)

This is a proverb. Ask yourself this question: Are there ever any exceptions to this proverb? The answer is . . . Yes, absolutely. Sometimes lazy people win the lottery or have a rich relative that dies and they inherit money. There are exceptions to this proverb. But as a general rule, that's the way that life works. That's the nature of a proverb. If you don't understand how a proverb works and you want to make it into a law, you will get very frustrated by this book.

Here are a few more examples if you want to expand on this exercise:

· *Example 4:* "If we confess our sins, he is faithful and just and will forgive us our sins and purify us from all unrighteousness." (1 John 1:9) **Promise**
· *Example 5:* "You shall not murder." (Exodus 20:13) **Law**
· *Example 6:* "Do not answer a fool according to his folly, or you will be like him yourself." (Proverbs 26:4) **Proverb**

Ask an overcommitted person in our crazy society: "Is your hurried, frenzied, exhausting, self-preoccupied lifestyle producing in you the rivers of living water that Jesus promised would well up in the hearts of his followers?" They will admit that their insane lifestyle is robbing them of all they want most.

We keep doing things that we know are going to destroy us, but we can't seem to stop. Even when we identify the problem and resolve to change, we can find ourselves repeating the same sin over and over.

ILLUSTRATION | A Great Hymn

Many people grew up singing some of the great hymns of the church. One of them is entitled "My Jesus I Love Thee," which has a message we need to remember today. The hymn begins, "My Jesus, I love Thee. I know Thou art mine. For Thee *all the folly of sin I resign*." What an inspired phrase! What a great reminder! The proverbs were written to help us resign from the folly of sin.

3. Adopting a Proverb

As we conclude this message we are going to think practically about how proverbs can help shape and transform our lives. Proverbs cover many areas of life, but we are going to look at six specific proverbs and the life-transformation they call us to experience. The challenge will be for everybody gathered to adopt a proverb for the week.

After you pick a proverb, it would be wise to tell somebody else what your proverb of the week is. Invite them to pray for you as you seek to develop a wise lifestyle in this specific area. Also, commit to write your proverb down and put it someplace where you will see it often through the week. In addition, plan to memorize your proverb, as the early Jews did. Make this statement of wisdom your own and watch how it impacts your life.

NEW TESTAMENT CONNECTION

Paul Understood

The apostle Paul understood the battle of the soul and expressed his own struggle with sin and folly. He wrote: "I do not understand what I do. For what I want to do I do not do, but what I hate I do" (Romans 7:15).

ON THE LIGHTER SIDE | Why Do We Need Proverbs?

In ancient Israel the proverbs were an essential curriculum for everyday life. They helped people learn how to honor God. Young people memorized these words by the chapter. Not just a verse but a whole chapter! Why do you think God devoted an entire book of the Bible to words of wisdom? Here is the answer, and it has deep theological significance. It may not sound theological, but if you reflect on this truth, it will begin to make sense: *People are stupid!*

If you take nothing else away from this message, be sure to remember this truth. Let's say it out loud together: "*People are stupid.*" It is important to remember that this is not the whole truth about us, but it is an important part of the truth.

NARRATIVE ON THE TEXT | A Proverb About Our Words

Proverbs 10:19 is pretty straightforward. The more you talk, the more you sin. So, one of the simplest ways to cut down on sin is to stop talking so much. A wise person will refrain from speaking in many situations. Sometimes holding our tongue is the best way to show that we are growing in wisdom. Note, of course, that for a person given to silence (or who uses the "silent treatment"), this is not a text to hide behind, nor is this the text for such a one to choose to work on for this week.

LIFE APPLICATION | A Time for Silence

Henry Nouwen writes about the value of silence and learning to hold our tongue in a wonderful little book called *The Way of the Heart*. He tells about the early Christian wisdom figures who recommended that followers of Christ engage in the practice of silence. This is valuable for many reasons, but one of the most important is that it is hard to talk without sinning.

Consider taking a vow of silence for an hour or set aside a whole day for silence. If your schedule does not allow you to take a full day, then try going a day where you only say what you must. Let your words be as few as possible. When you practice this discipline of silence, you will discover many amazing things. Here are some of the lessons learned in silence:

- You can live without getting in the last word in every situation.

- You can survive without trying to make sure you control how everybody else thinks about you.

SIGNIFICANT SCRIPTURE

Proverbs 10:19
*When words are many,
sin is not absent,
but he who holds his
tongue is wise.*

ON THE LIGHTER SIDE | What About Contradictory Proverbs?

Another aspect of Proverbs that can confuse people is that sometimes they sound as if they contradict each other. Since proverbs are not absolute laws, this should not bother us too much. But, to help make sense of this, let's think about how modern proverbs also often seem to contradict each other, and this does not seem to bother us. Think about these pairings of contemporary proverbs:

"Look before you leap," *and* "He who hesitates is lost."
"Opposites attract," *and* "Birds of a feather flock together."
"Absence makes the heart grow fonder," *and* "Out of sight, out of mind."
"Many hands make light work," *and* "Too many cooks spoil the soup."

"You have to keep your eye on the ball," *and* "A watched pot never boils."

What's going on here? The fact is, every proverb addresses one limited slice of reality. They are written to help people avoid folly, and people often err in opposite extremes. The proverb we need to focus on depends on our own tendencies and weaknesses.

For example, think about "Look before you leap," *and* "He who hesitates is lost." People who tend to be impulsive need to heed the first of these two, while those who can never seem to make up their mind need to hear the second one.

- You don't have to win every argument.

- Other people have great ideas and insights and can figure things out without your input.

- You can go for days without drawing attention to yourself.

As you learn the wisdom of silence, you may discover that there is a new and better way to live. Of course the goal is not to stop talking. The discipline of silence is a tool to help you listen more, choose your words more carefully, and to lower the sin level in your life.

NARRATIVE ON THE TEXT | A Proverb about Laziness

Proverbs 19:24 depicts a caricature of a person who is lazy. He puts his hand in the nacho bowl and decides it's not worth the energy it will take to transport the food to his mouth. He thinks, "It's too much work. I'll just leave my hand right there. Maybe the wind will blow one of the nachos my way." The point is that no one is ever nurtured by laziness. Lack of action always leads to loss of life. God wants us to use our energy, strength, and abilities for his glory.

LIFE APPLICATION | Battling Laziness

For those who wrestle with passivity, procrastination, inertia, or apathy, Proverbs 19:24 may be one they want to adopt. If this strikes a chord for you, then identify one area of life where you are struggling with procrastination. What will it take for you to move into action in this area? Who can keep you accountable? What can you do to battle laziness and begin to take specific steps forward toward transformation in this area of your life?

NARRATIVE ON THE TEXT | A Proverb about Enduring

Proverbs 10:25 acknowledges the fact that storms do come in life. The question is not if, but when! Yet, at the end of the day, God helps the righteous stand strong. Even in the toughest of times, we can rest assured that God will be with his people. For those who are facing times that demand endurance, faith, and a steadfast spirit, this is a great proverb for them.

LIFE APPLICATION | Stand Strong

Some of you who are listening to this message are right in the middle of a storm. You are in desperate need of a word of encouragement that gives hope that when the storm passes, your house will still be standing. Maybe you have been abandoned or betrayed. You're going through a divorce. You have been wiped out by a financial disaster. You've lost your job. Somebody you love has died. You have a child you're so worried about that you can't sleep at night. You are battling depression and can't seem to pull yourself out of it. Some days you even wonder if you can make it.

If this describes you, Proverbs 10:25 may be your proverb. It does not give an easy answer or even a guarantee that everything will be better by tomorrow morning. What it does give is hope that when the storm passes, those who cling to God will still be standing. As you meditate on this proverb, you will be encouraged to say, "I'm not going to let go. I don't care how bad the storm is. It will be over one day in this life or the next, and I will still be standing."

NARRATIVE ON THE TEXT | A Proverb about Discipline

We all need to hear the unvarnished truth from people who love us. A wise person listens and learns from these words of discipline. A fool ignores and resists loving correction. If we are going to become the people God wants us to be, we need to become humble enough to accept and even invite discipline. If we only surround ourselves with people who agree with us and affirm everything we do, we will never grow. Proverbs gives this powerful word of wisdom: "Wounds from a friend can be trusted, but an enemy multiplies kisses" (Proverbs 27:6).

ILLUSTRATION | Who Can I Learn From?

In Numbers 22 we read the story of Balaam and his donkey. Balaam was instructed and corrected by his donkey. What a lesson for all of us. If Balaam could learn from a donkey, then God can certainly teach us through all kinds of people. If we are humble and listen, God wants to instruct us through the most surprising of people.

LIFE APPLICATION | A Listening Ear and Receptive Heart

This may seem like a strange thing to say, but one sign that you are growing in spiritual maturity is that you humbly receive criticism. This does not mean every criticism is right or that you have to agree with it. However, a listening ear and a receptive heart honors God. It might be time for you to ask God to soften your heart and help you receive correction. You may even be able to identify specific people God has been using to speak correction into your life, but you have been resisting. Let this be the time you begin accepting, or even inviting, their words.

NEW TESTAMENT CONNECTION

A House Built on a Rock

Which of Jesus' parables does Proverbs 10:25 remind you of? Do you remember the parable about the house built on the rock and the house built on the sand in Matthew 7:24-27? When a storm came, the house on the sand was blown away, but the house on the rock stood firm. The parable in Matthew is an elaborated version of this proverb.

SIGNIFICANT SCRIPTURE

Proverbs 12:1
Whoever loves discipline loves knowledge,

but he who hates correction is stupid.

NARRATIVE ON THE TEXT | A Proverb about Selfishness

Have you ever seen a leech? They are natural-born bloodsuckers. They attach onto a host body with both ends of their little bodies; that's where the idea of "two daughters" comes from. These two daughters both say, "Give! Give!" Because the leech is a taker, it is never expected to give anything back. A leech never hooks onto you and says, "I have a gift I'd like to give to you." Leeches only make withdrawals, never deposits. Proverbs 30:15 is pointing to people who take and take and never learn to give. Clearly, they are not walking in the way of wisdom.

SIGNIFICANT SCRIPTURE
Proverbs 30:15

The leech has two daughters.
"Give! Give!" they cry.
There are three things that are never satisfied,
four that never say, "Enough!"

LIFE APPLICATION | Taming the Leech in Us

It is possible for the human spirit to become leech-like in its selfishness. So much in our culture dictates in this direction. Television commercials and magazine ads encourage self-centered living. A lot of bright folks stay up at night figuring out ways to grow in leech-like living. Jesus also gave many warnings about the power of things and the human propensity for always wanting more. If Proverbs 10:15 connects for you, it may be time to begin identifying behavior in your life that has a "give-me, feed-me" feeling to it. As God begins to show you areas of life where you are always wanting and demanding more, submit these to him and pray for a content and generous spirit.

LIFE APPLICATION | A Proverb about Generosity

SIGNIFICANT SCRIPTURE
Proverbs 19:17

He who is kind to the poor lends to the LORD,
and he will reward him for what he has done.

If you are kind to the poor, it's like lending to God. Maybe the generosity factor in your life needs to be turned up a notch. What better thing can you do with your resources than share with the poor and be generous toward God? Maybe Proverbs 19:17 is the proverb you need to take with you as you ask God to help you develop a generous spirit.

CREATIVE MESSAGE IDEA | Share It

Invite everyone to turn to someone around them and reveal which proverb they have adopted. First, tell them which proverb hit home for you. Second, share how you feel God wants to impact your life through this proverb. Finally, let them know how they can pray for you as you seek to adopt this proverb and see it impact your life.

DEUTERONOMY 17:14-20; 1 KINGS 3; 9:1-9; 10:14-29; 11:1-13

The Heart of the
MESSAGE

How does a person go from being the wisest man on the earth to a man buried neck deep in folly? How does a person move from being sensitive toward God to living a life of radical disobedience?

The truth is, nobody sets out to experience this kind of fall—least of all Solomon. If you asked him early in his life and kingship, "Solomon, do you think you will stray from the path of wisdom and end up living like a fool?" he would have been shocked. But that is exactly what happened.

In this session we will focus on how a person can move from wisdom to folly, and we will seek to identify ways to stop this process before we go too far. There are decisions that get made all along the way that can help or hinder us. There are steps we can take in our journey of faith that have the potential to ruin even the best of people and lead them into the depths of folly.

The Heart of the
MESSENGER

Solomon's life is a road map we might call, "The way to disaster"! In this session we will see four detours he took that led him from wisdom to folly. As a leader, you have the opportunity to study this lesson in advance and see if you have begun walking on the road to foolishness. Take time to reflect on each of the four detours Solomon took and ask God to help you see if you are headed toward wisdom or folly. If you see areas where wisdom is growing in your life, thank God for this and pray for the power to stay on the right path. If the Holy Spirit alerts you to ways you are walking the path of foolishness, seek to repent and turn from these ways. Even the wisest of people can be enticed to walk in the way of fools. Let this be an opportunity for you to make sure your feet are on the right path.

Brief Message
OUTLINE

1. The Road from Extreme Wisdom to Extreme Folly

2. Step 1: Allowing a Little Wiggle Room

3. Step 2: Assuming You Are the Exception

4. Step 3: Failing to Deal with Predisposed Weaknesses

5. Step 4: Ignoring Correction

1. The Road from Extreme Wisdom to Extreme Folly

ILLUSTRATION | From the Height of a Wedding to the Depth of Divorce

In his message (on the OTC audio CD), Tim Schroeder tells about his experience of seeing the joy of a wedding and the deep pain of divorce. His story is recorded below and can be used as a sermon illustration. If you have your own story about the dramatic contrast you have seen between a happy marriage and a tragic divorce, you may want to tell it at the start of this message.

A pastor tells about the height of a wedding and the depth of divorce:

Some years ago I stood at the front of our church and was able to share in one of the most special moments a young man and woman can experience. There they stood, wearing the nicest clothes they might ever put on. They stood and faced each other, joined hands, and looked deeply into each other's eyes. They spoke vows with absolute sincerity. They said, "In the presence of God and before all of these people, I promise my love to you. I commit to love, cherish, and honor you. I'll be faithful to you. As long as my heart beats, I give it to you." In that sacred moment, they were married in the sight of God.

When I got home, my wife asked, "How was the wedding?" I said, "You know, there's that one moment in all weddings that is just so special. It's so sacred. What a highlight in life. What an unforgettable moment!"

This pastor was bivocational and also worked as a police officer. Later that same evening he changed into his police uniform and went on duty. At about 10:00 that evening he was called to a domestic dispute. When he arrived, there were already a couple of squad cars on the scene. Several policemen were in the kitchen restraining the husband and the wife who were screaming and shouting obscenities at each other.

They clearly didn't need any more officers in there, so he went into the living room and looked around. As he was surveying the scene, he noticed that the wall unit had been pulled over and smashed. The television and stereo were on the floor. Plants were uprooted and there was dirt from one end of the room to the other. As he stood there surveying the damage, something caught his attention out of the corner of his eye—something moved.

A little girl and boy were coming out from behind the sofa where they had been hiding. The girl was three years old and her little brother was about eighteen months old. They walked right up to this pastor-policeman and the little boy just put up his arms as if to invite the officer to pick him up. The little girl said, "Mister, can you hold my brother? He's scared."

As the officer picked that little guy up and held him close, he turned his face so that no one would walk in and see him. At that moment tears began to stream down his face as he held this brokenhearted little boy and looked down into the scared face of his sister. He stood there bawling and wondering, *How does that happen?* How does anybody go from a vibrant, wonderful declaration of love, where all marriages begin, to a nightmare of disillusionment and sorrow?

SIGNIFICANT
SCRIPTURE

1 Kings 3

NARRATIVE ON THE TEXT | A Quick Review

In 1 Kings 3 we see Solomon at his best. God appeared to him and asked him to request anything he wanted. As we learned in the last session, Solomon asked for wisdom—and he got it in spades! God poured amazing wisdom into Solomon's heart and also blessed him with riches, honor, and military victories. It seemed as if Solomon had everything.

Later in this chapter we read of Solomon's most famous display of wisdom. Two prostitutes were sleeping, and one of their babies was smothered during the night. In the morning, the woman whose child had died switched the babies. When they brought the one baby to Solomon, each one claimed it was hers. Solomon gave that wisest of all decisions and ended up placing the baby in the arms of the true mother. In response, the people were in awe of his wisdom.

From there Solomon went on to a season of great wisdom, fame, accomplishments, and approval. God celebrated his choices and wisdom, and so did the people. Sadly, the story did not end there. Solomon, who began as an amazing example of wisdom, ended up falling into a bottomless pit of foolishness.

INTERPRETIVE INSIGHT | A Chilling Irony

We cannot miss the chilling irony of what's being said here. Solomon began his career with a wise decision that became legendary. That decision restored a live baby to its mother. He ended his career by worshiping a god to whom child sacrifices were made by their own parents.

SIGNIFICANT
SCRIPTURE

1 Kings 11:1-13

HISTORICAL CONTEXT | Ashtoreth and Molech

In 1 Kings 11 we see Solomon at the end of his life. Rather than a celebration of his wisdom, we read a chronicle of his foolish choices and how these choices impacted those around him. Some of the most chilling words about Solomon are found in 1 Kings 11:4-6:

As Solomon grew old, his wives turned his heart after other gods, and his heart was not fully devoted to the LORD his God, as the heart of David his father had

been. He followed Ashtoreth the goddess of the Sidonians, and Molech the detestable god of the Ammonites. So Solomon did evil in the eyes of the LORD; he did not follow the LORD completely, as David his father had done.

How did Solomon go from extreme wisdom to such blatant disobedience in a few brief chapters? In these verses we learn that Solomon followed Ashtoreth. She was a Canaanite fertility goddess.

This false deity was closely connected to cultic temple prostitution that degraded people and greatly offended God. We also read that Solomon followed Molech, the "detestable" god of the Ammonite people. Molech was another false god, but there was a particularly hideous aspect to Molech worship: He was given human sacrifices. The Ammonites and others who followed Molech were expected to sacrifice their infants to him on his altar.

2. The Downward Spiral: Step 1—Allowing a Little Wiggle Room

The first step in Solomon's downward spiral was to leave a little wiggle room in his commitment. It all began with areas of compromise that many people may have thought were not that important. Of course, a little wiggle room became a lot of wiggle room in a short time.

NARRATIVE ON LIFE | ## The Problem with Partial Obedience

Israel was commanded to have nothing to do with the high places except to destroy them. However, with some regularity, instead of demolishing them, especially before the temple was constructed, the Israelites converted some of them to shrines and began worshiping God there.

They tried to fit in with the religious culture of that day. People from the nation of Israel would go to these pagan high places but instead of worshiping idols, they attempted to worship the one true God. They meant well. They had good intentions. And God didn't strike them down. In fact, sometimes, confusing as it may be, in his mercy, God even met them there.

It is important that all followers of Christ understand what was happening when the people of Israel tried to adopt these pagan places of worship. Even though they had good intentions, even though God didn't punish them immediately, they were *still not fully obedient*. Good intentions are never a substitute for obedience. The people were not separating themselves totally from pagan idolatry. God had commanded them to have nothing to do with these high places, but they decided to dabble a little bit. They allowed just a little wiggle room, and it cost them dearly. This was exactly how Solomon got his start.

SIGNIFICANT SCRIPTURE

1 Kings 3:1-3

WORD STUDY

"Except"

In 1 Kings 3:3 we read: "Solomon showed his love for the LORD by walking according to the statutes of his father David, *except that he offered sacrifices and burned incense on the high places.*" What's the key word in this verse? "Except"! When we read the word "except," we know Solomon is in trouble. Once we hear this word, we don't even need to know what comes next. This word is a clear indicator that Solomon has decided to leave some wiggle room in his devotion. He will try to love God and be devoted, except for a few areas.

HISTORICAL CONTEXT | ### Destroy the High Places

Solomon's area of wiggle room was this, "except that he offered sacrifices and burned incense on the high places." There's a lot of confusion surrounding these high places in the Old Testament. For one thing, they were almost always associated with pagan worship and idolatry. Numerous times Israel was told that they were supposed to demolish and utterly destroy the high places. In Numbers 33:51-52 this issue is addressed with clarity:

Speak to the Israelites and say to them: "When you cross the Jordan into Canaan, drive out all the inhabitants of the land before you. Destroy all their carved images and their cast idols, and demolish all their high places."

In Deuteronomy 33:29 the people are blessed because they will trample down the "high places."

Blessed are you, O Israel!
   Who is like you,
   a people saved by the LORD?

He is your shield and helper
   and your glorious sword.
Your enemies will cower before you,
   and you will trample down their high places.

Clearly God did not want the remains of false pagan worship to remain in the land. The people were to get rid of it and avoid all practices related to what God had declared an abomination.

He followed what God commanded, except . . .

He had good intentions, except . . .

Like Solomon, we can be tempted to cover up disobedience with good intentions. But we must learn the lesson Solomon faced: Leaving a little wiggle room is one of the most dangerous steps in the downward spiral from wisdom to folly. Leaving a little wiggle room in our commitment to God almost always leads to a little more wiggle room.

LIFE APPLICATION | 95 Percent Devotion Is 5 Percent Short!

There is no such thing as partial commitment. When you begin with an exception clause, you never arrive at full devotion. A good life lesson for all followers of Christ is that 95 percent devotion to God is 5 percent short. God calls us to a complete surrender to his leading in our lives. He does not do this to take away our fun or limit our freedom. He calls us to full devotion because he knows we will find fullness of joy and true freedom when we are 100 percent devoted to him.

We need to look honestly at our lives and ask some hard questions:

- Where am I allowing wiggle room in my devotion to God?

- How am I being tempted to wander from God because of the areas where I am allowing wiggle room?

- What are some of the consequences I might face if I keep allowing this wiggle room in my life?

- What is it going to take for me to be 100 percent devoted in this area of my life?

When we leave any wiggle room in our commitment to God, we are leaving the door open for disaster. If we leave it open just a crack, sooner or later the wind will blow it all the way. Solomon got started with a little wiggle room and ended up in radical disobedience. If we are not careful, we can see history repeat itself in our lives.

ON THE LIGHTER SIDE
Don't Try This at Home

Don't try this one at home, it will never fly! Can you imagine a husband coming to his wife and saying, "Honey, I love you and I promise to be faithful to you, except. . . ." What can he say after that that is going to make any difference at all? The simple fact that he says "except" is a guarantee that he will be in deep water.

HISTORICAL CONTEXT | Stay Away from Egypt

As we read more of 1 Kings 3, we see that Solomon made a few more exceptions. Solomon actually had a military and political alliance with Pharaoh, the king of Egypt, and Solomon married Pharaoh's daughter. We might be baffled by this. Why would the king of Israel make this kind of pact with the king of Egypt?

The people of Israel had been specifically commanded *not* to intermarry with people who worshiped foreign gods.

Moreover, God had warned them to stay away from Egypt and any alliance with the Egyptians. He had delivered his people from Egypt and wanted them to avoid the Egyptians at all costs.

3. The Downward Spiral: Step 2—Assuming You Are the Exception to the Rule

Step 2 in the downward spiral from wisdom to folly is to assume that you are the exception to the rule. You are above God's rules. At this point in the spiral, you don't dispute the rules. You don't disagree with them. In fact, you agree that they're fine for most people. But you just think that you're a little more mature and a little more sophisticated than others. You can handle it. You don't have to follow God's rules as closely as everybody else does.

The problem with anything less than total obedience is that you're the one who then gets to choose what you will submit to and what "really doesn't matter." In a sense, when this happens, you have become your own king. You have become your own god.

NARRATIVE ON THE TEXT | Three Strikes for Solomon

SIGNIFICANT SCRIPTURE

Deuteronomy 17:14-20;
1 Kings 10:14-29

Solomon began with a little wiggle room. Before too long, he was rewriting the rule book! Take note of how many ways Solomon began to break God's clear commands. In each of these areas Solomon may have felt that God's rules were good and should be obeyed, but somehow they just did not apply to him and his situation.

Look closely at some of the detailed and specific commands God gave to those who would rule over his people. Look at Deuteronomy 17:16–17 (italics added):

> The king, moreover, must *not acquire great numbers of horses* for himself or make the people return to *Egypt* to get more of them, for the LORD has told you, "You are not to go back that way again." He must *not take many wives*, or his heart will be led astray. He *must not accumulate large amounts of silver and gold.*

ON THE LIGHTER SIDE | In the G.I. Lab

Have you ever heard of a G.I. nurse? This is a nurse who works in a specialized discipline of medicine. If you don't know what a gastrointestinal nurse is, you should go home, get on your knees, and say a prayer of thanks to God!

The G.I. lab in a hospital is not a nice place. One of the jobs of a G.I. nurse is to sterilize all of the scopes and instruments. What would happen if a nurse decided that the scopes did not need to be fully sterile? This would be a disaster! There is no such thing as a partially sterile scope. It's either sterile or it's not. If there's one germ alive, it's contaminated.

In Solomon's life he let a couple germs live, and they infected his whole life. In a G.I. lab, every germ needs to be destroyed. In our spiritual lives, we need to be sure that we are 100 percent devoted.

This seems pretty clear:

- no horses from Egypt

- not too many wives

- no large amounts of wealth

But, Solomon did not think all of these commands applied to him. Just look at what transpired in his life. It is important to note that the specific commands given three centuries earlier were all broken by Solomon. When these are listed in 1 Kings 10, they show up in essentially the same order as they were given in Deuteronomy. What an indictment of Solomon's rebellious heart in 1 Kings 10:26–11:3!

> Solomon accumulated chariots and horses; *he had fourteen hundred chariots and twelve thousand horses*, which he kept in the chariot cities and also with him in Jerusalem. The king *made silver as common in Jerusalem as stones*, and cedar as plentiful as sycamore-fig trees in the foothills. Solomon's horses were *imported from Egypt.* . . .
> King Solomon, however, loved many foreign women besides Pharaoh's daughter. . . . They were from nations about which the LORD had told the Israelites, "You must not intermarry with them, because they will surely turn your hearts after their gods." Nevertheless, Solomon held fast to them in love. He had *seven hundred wives of royal birth and three hundred concubines*, and his wives led him astray.

God commanded the kings of Israel to stay away from any arms build-up that would give them the tendency to rely on their own power and not on God.

ON THE LIGHTER SIDE **98 Percent to Jesus I Surrender**

There is an old hymn of the church that many people sang as they grew up. The title of this song is "I Surrender All." The chorus goes like this:

> I surrender all,
> I surrender all,
> All to Thee, my blessed Savior,
> I surrender all.

Do you get the message? Is it clear? This is a declaration of absolute, complete, uncompromising devotion. Can you imagine a congregation of Christians gathered and singing this song but lowering the bar just a little? What might they sing? How might they rewrite the song?

- Most to Jesus, I Surrender
- Some to Jesus, I Surrender
- 98 Percent to Jesus, I Surrender

The only thing that makes sense and fits with God's call on our lives is full devotion. We need to declare, "*All to Jesus, I surrender.*" Then, we need to do it!

One of the first things Solomon did was strike a treaty with the king of Egypt by marrying an Egyptian wife, and he bought twelve thousand horses, most of which were from Egypt. Strike one! God told the kings to avoid amassing wealth. He wanted them to rely on his provision and not their own stockpile. But Solomon made silver as common as rocks in the street. Strike two! God said to avoid having too many wives, and Solomon went on to set a world record with seven hundred. A big strike three!

NARRATIVE ON LIFE | From Blessing to Greed

One thing we must remember is that God did promise he would bless Solomon with riches. But Solomon did what so many people do: He turned blessing into greed. He was consumed by the blessing. He got more and more and more and more, but he was never satisfied. He never had enough. Instead of growing in contentment, he wanted more, and along the way he started to violate every law that God had given for the kings.

Solomon started out by saying, "I don't know what I'm doing. I need your wisdom," though he left just a little bit of wiggle room. Then, once he got up and was flying high, he started to think, "I can get horses from Egypt. I can get more money. I can marry whomever I want." God's blessings became Solomon's license for greed, and it took over his life.

ILLUSTRATION | The One Thing the Church Can't Handle

Tony Campolo, a Christian speaker and author, was once asked, "What do you see as the biggest challenge facing the church today?" His response might surprise you:

> When I look at the church today, especially in America, I see that the church is doing quite well. The church is flourishing. The church has power in a lot of areas. It has a lot of wealth. It's

HISTORICAL CONTEXT | Lots of Gold!

We are told that Solomon received 666 talents of gold as a regular payment (1 Kings 10:14). This was just from one source of his income. Did you ever wonder how much gold that was? The basic conversion is that a talent was seventy-five pounds. If you do the math, you will discover that he was approaching eight hundred thousand ounces of gold from just one income stream. The value of gold changes, but it can float around $290 an ounce. At this rate the value of this one income source was about 232 million dollars a year. That's a lot of money.

doing really well! And, it terrifies me because throughout history, there is one thing the church has never been able to handle . . . success!

He went on to say:

> The church has always thrived in times of persecution. It's done really well when it had hardship placed upon it. But, the church has failed every time it's had power and wealth—every time. The church seems to handle everything except success.

LIFE APPLICATION | The Humility Quotient

Solomon started out asking God for help. He saw his need and weaknesses and relied on God. As soon as he got a few things going his way, he got too big for his britches. He started thinking he could choose what he would obey and what he would not.

How's your humility quotient? Are you growing more humble as the years pass? Do you pray for humility and seek to keep pride out of your heart? One of the purposes behind humility is that it is difficult to obey if you are arrogant. It is difficult to submit if you think you know better. So how are you doing on the humility side—step two of the equation?

4. The Downward Spiral: Step 3—Failing to Deal with Predisposed Weaknesses

Step 3 in the downward spiral from wisdom to folly is failing to deal with predisposed weaknesses. We all have them. But when we refuse to look at them and resist turning away from them, we are headed for trouble.

NARRATIVE ON THE TEXT | He Loved Women

In 1 Kings 11:1–2 we read that Solomon had an insatiable love for women:

> King Solomon, however, loved many foreign women besides Pharaoh's daughter—Moabites, Ammonites, Edomites, Sidonians and Hittites. They were from nations about which the LORD had told the Israelites, "You must not intermarry with them, because they will surely turn your hearts after their gods."

Clearly Solomon was crossing the line. These were women whom God had forbidden the Israelites to marry. The reason for his command to avoid these women is also explicit. They would turn the heart of their husband toward false gods and idols.

NEW TESTAMENT CONNECTION

God Loves Humility!

Throughout the New Testament we are reminded that God loves for his children to walk in humility. He also has a real problem with those who are ruled by pride! This truth, which is expressed so clearly in the Old Testament, is reinforced again and again in the New Testament:

> God opposes the proud but gives grace to the humble. (This is from Proverbs 3:34 and is quoted in both James 4:6 and 1 Peter 5:5.)

> Do not be proud, but be willing to associate with people of low position. Do not be conceited. (Romans 12:16)

> Be completely humble and gentle; be patient, bearing with one another in love. (Ephesians 4:2)

SIGNIFICANT SCRIPTURE

1 Kings 11:1–8

WORD STUDY

"Nevertheless"

When we read the end of 1 Kings 11:2, we come across one of the saddest words recorded about Solomon's life. It is the word "nevertheless." This word jumps off the page as we read it and see what follows. Solomon's "nevertheless" attitude and actions led to his downfall.

Nevertheless, Solomon held fast to them in love. He had seven hundred wives of royal birth and three hundred concubines, and his wives led him astray. As Solomon grew old, his wives turned his heart after other gods, and his heart was not fully devoted to the LORD his God, as the heart of David his father had been. He followed Ashtoreth the goddess of the Sidonians, and Molech the detestable god of the Ammonites. So Solomon did evil in the eyes of the LORD; he did not follow the LORD completely, as David his father had done. (1 Kings 11:2–6)

Solomon knew that what he was doing was wrong. This wasn't just a little rule about some gold and horses from Egypt. God had made it crystal clear that his people were to avoid those who worshiped false gods and idols. God warned them that unbelieving spouses could become a snare to them. Sadly, that is exactly what happened in Solomon's life.

LIFE APPLICATION | Nevertheless Moments

Solomon said, "Nevertheless . . ." even when he knew what he was doing was wrong. He just went on and did it anyway. It was as if he could not help himself. His attraction to women was a battle he would fight his entire life.

Have you ever known someone who could not seem to help himself or herself when it came to a certain sin? Have you ever been that person? Are you in that situation right now? Sometimes sin gets a grip on our life and it feels as if we can't get away. We feel enticed or tempted, we know it is wrong, but we end up saying, "Nevertheless."

When this happens, God wants us to look to him for strength. Even if we feel that there is no way we can resist, God wants us to know that there is. Remember the reminder in 1 Corinthians 10:13, "No temptation has seized you except what is common to man. And God is faithful; he will not let you be tempted beyond what you can bear. But when you are tempted, he will also provide a way out so that you can stand up under it."

There is one other life application note that should be made here. Followers of Christ today still need to hear God's warning about marrying someone who is not a committed believer. Many Christians today still say, "Nevertheless" and go on to marry a man or woman who is not a devoted follower of Jesus. This can bring many heartaches and struggles in life. We need to make sure, before we go too far in a relationship, that the other person is deeply committed to Jesus.

NARRATIVE ON THE TEXT | Deep in the Family System

Solomon was not particularly discriminating when it came to women. He seemed to love them all! Even when God gave clear commands about this, he kept right on marrying women who were forbidden. We have to stop and wonder why he struggled so much in this area of his life.

When we look back through Solomon's personal history, some clues begin to rise to the surface. Let's ask a few questions. Who was Solomon's dad? David. Who was his mother? Bathsheba. Does anything jump to mind about why Solomon might have had a problem with sexual control when you think of his parents? It is clear that David struggled with sexual temptation, and his choices and lifestyle seem to have impacted his son.

Solomon had been exposed to sexual struggles through his whole life. If you read through the Old Testament, you discover that David's family had one of the most dysfunctional households around. There is a very good chance that Solomon's problems stretched all the way to David's bedroom. The sins and weaknesses of his father infected his life and impacted him for a lifetime!

LIFE APPLICATION | Shaping Our Children's Future

Parents, do you have any idea of the die you are casting for your children? You are shaping and building habits into their lives that will impact them more than you dream. Their outlooks, strengths, weaknesses, and attitudes will be shaped by your life. If you have kids in your home, they are watching you. They are learning. They are being shaped. For better or for worse, you are forming their lives.

With this in mind, we must do a serious evaluation of our own attitudes and actions. There are lots of questions we need to ask. Here are a few to get us started:

- What are the hidden attitudes in you that you do not want passed on to your children and grandchildren?

- What habits do you have that you hope and pray your children will not adopt as their own?

- What are the secret and hidden sins that you work to keep your children from knowing about?

Too often we live with a level of self-deceit. We think our attitudes, actions, and hidden sins go unnoticed by our children. But we are wrong. They do know. They can see it, smell it, and feel it! Our sins do impact them, no matter how much we try to avoid it.

Do you really think your children and grandchildren don't know about that stuff you've got stashed away in the basement, attic, garage, or some corner at home? You can't even hide their Christmas presents where they can't find them. And kids know how to check the history of computer searches and files better than you do.

With the Spirit of God as your guide, take time for self-examination today! Ask yourself, what am I passing on to my kids? What are the areas of weakness in my own life, the predisposed weaknesses that I'm handing on to another generation?

Then, commit, with all of God's strength, to make the cycle of sin end with your generation! If you need to get a strong Christian accountability partner, do it! If you need to meet with a church leader, do it! If you need to get help from a Christian counselor, take action immediately. But whatever you do, don't pass your sin on to the next generation.

An Honest Look at My History

Before moving on to the final portion of this message, pause to pray. This third part of the spiritual spiral downward hits some very tender nerves. Pray for the Holy Spirit to illuminate and reveal areas of sin. Ask for power for God's people to change their life attitudes and patterns. Offer confession for how their lives may have damaged the next generation, and lift up thanks for those in the previous generation who have passed on the blessing of a godly heritage.

SIGNIFICANT SCRIPTURE

1 Kings 9:1–9

ILLUSTRATION | For Better and For Worse

One piece of good news is that our good habits and attitudes also get passed on to the next generation. On the OTC sermon CD, Tim tells a story of his father's godly example and how it impacted his life. If you have a story about someone who passed on a healthy and positive spiritual legacy, you may want to tell it at this time.

5. The Downward Spiral: Step 4—Ignoring Correction

The final step on this downward spiral is to ignore or to silence corrective words. This is one of the surest signs of disaster. When a person is sliding down into sin and rebellion and he or she refuses to listen to anyone who comes with wise and loving correction, disaster is ready to strike. When a person has already gone through steps one, two, and three, sin has a way of deafening one's ears so he or she has a difficult time hearing God's voice.

NARRATIVE ON THE TEXT | A Loving Warning

In 1 Kings 9:1–2 Solomon had completed one of the high points in his life and career. He had finished and dedicated the temple. We read that God appeared to him again: "When Solomon had finished building the temple of the LORD and the royal palace, and had achieved all he had desired to do, the LORD appeared to him a second time, *as he had appeared to him at Gibeon*." It was at Gibeon (1 Kings 3:5) that God had appeared to Solomon and invited him to ask for whatever he wanted. Do you remember what Solomon asked of God? For wisdom! That was all. Since then, Solomon had become a very different man.

This time when God appears to Solomon at Gibeon, he comes with a warning. In effect, God says, "If you follow me, I will bless you. But if you refuse to follow me, I will cut you off!" God knows the condition of Solomon's life and heart, and it is time for a firm warning. Solomon is on a crash-course to disaster, so God steps in with a warning.

NARRATIVE ON THE TEXT | Two Men . . . Two Responses

As time passed, Solomon wandered farther and farther from God. He did not listen to warnings but did things his own way. God continued to call Solomon to a place of repentance, but he refused to respond. God raised up Jeroboam, a trusted servant of Solomon who knew the hearts of the people and was aware that the nation could end up being divided if things did not change. But Solomon remained hardhearted. We read words that are shocking: "Solomon tried to kill

Jeroboam, but Jeroboam fled to Egypt, to Shishak the king, and stayed there until Solomon's death" (1 Kings 11:40).

This is the difference between David and Solomon. When Nathan came and corrected David for his sin with Bathsheba, David got on his face, repented, and cried out to God, "How could I? Create in me a clean heart." Solomon tried to kill the messenger.

Our hearts should be open to correction. We need to humbly listen when God speaks and calls us to change. Our defense mechanisms can be turned up so high that we have a hard time hearing corrective words from God or his servants. But we must resist this tendency and learn to soften our hearts and open our ears.

PAUSE FOR PRAYER

Need Your Grace!

Take time to pray for God to break the downward spiral from wisdom to folly. If Solomon could fall into this pattern, none of us is exempt! Pray for the power of God's Holy Spirit to fill each person as we learn to break the cycle of pride and sin and grow in humble obedience.

Job: Where Is God When It Hurts?

THE BOOK OF JOB

The Heart of the
MESSAGE

Many people think the book of Job is all about Job. The reality is, it is all about God! In this powerful drama, God reveals much about himself. Along the way we learn a lot about ourselves, but the center of this book is God. He is in control, he made everything, he delights in the creation, and he can be trusted. This book addresses the reality of suffering in life, but most of all, it gives us a window into the heart and character of God.

The Heart of the
MESSENGER

Job is a remarkable book. Studying it invariably involves a steep learning curve for anyone who really digs and wants to learn. As you prepare to bring this message, get ready to meet with God. Specifically, take time to read Job 38–41 and reflect on the questions God asks Job. Listen to these words as if they were written to you. Then, prepare your message with a heart saturated with the reality of who God is and what he has done.

Brief Message
OUTLINE

1. Setting the Scene
2. The Drama Unfolds
3. The Characters Speak
4. The Epilogue

1. Setting the Scene

NARRATIVE ON LIFE | ### Job's Story Is Our Story

The problems in the book of Job are the problems of the human race. They're the problems we all face. We can all see ourselves in the story of Job.

In the beginning, everything is as we think it should be. Job is a pious man. He is so cautious that he even offers sacrifices for his children just in case they have done something wrong that he does not know about. He wonders if God might be easily offended, and he takes no chances.

God has given him a wonderful life. He is the richest man in the east, the greatest man in his land. The amount of blessing he experiences seems to be directly proportional to the amount of obedience he offers toward God.

INTERPRETIVE INSIGHT | ### A Place of Unplanned Suffering

Trouble is coming to the land of Uz. Job does not know it, he is not expecting it, but it is coming like a tsunami. Uz will be a place where very bad things happen to a very good man. Uz will be a place where suffering comes with no warning and with no explanation. This suffering will create confusion and despair beyond words.

The hard truth is that everybody will spend some time in the land of Uz. And some people are there right now. Others have just traveled through and still feel the aftermath. Others don't know it, but the land of Uz is directly ahead.

ILLUSTRATION | ### A Play on Two Levels

As we study Job, it may help to compare it to a play. It is written that way. Think of a play in which there are two stages. There is an upper stage that is built high on risers and is near the ceiling of the theater. On that stage is the activity that takes place in heaven. The people on the upper stage can look down and see what is happening on the stage below. But there is also a lower stage, which features the activity taking place on earth. Those on the lower stage can't see what is happening above them on the upper stage.

HISTORICAL CONTEXT | ### Where Was Uz?

The story of Job begins in the land of Uz. What we have to do is try to figure out where Uz was. We know that it was east, but east of what? The answer is, east of Israel. The point of this is that Job was not from Israel. He wasn't one of God's special nation. This is quite a unique book in that it does not involve the history of Israel.

INTERPRETIVE INSIGHT | A Limited Perspective

We, as the readers (those watching the drama unfold), are able to see what's happening on both stages—upper and lower. This is crucial to the story. We know what's going on in both settings. We must remember, however, that the characters on earth (the lower stage) do not have our vantage point. They are aware of the activity around them but not above them. They know nothing about what's happening on the higher stage. They have a limited perspective, but we see everything as it unfolds.

2. The Drama Unfolds

NARRATIVE ON THE TEXT | How Do You Respond to Deep Loss?

In this portion of Job, Satan appears on the upper stage, in heaven, but then he moves to the lower stage. When he does, Job loses everything. He is pummeled with loss, pain, and heartache. Job's livestock, wealth, servants, and children are all swept away! When this happens, we see Job's response (Job 1:20–22):

> At this, Job got up and tore his robe and shaved his head. Then
> he fell to the ground in worship and said:
>
> > "Naked I came from my mother's womb,
> >   and naked I will depart.
> > The LORD gave and the LORD has taken away;
> >   may the name of the LORD be praised."
>
> In all this, Job did not sin by charging God with wrongdoing.

We learn that Job grieves and expresses it in outward ways that were common in his day. He tore his clothing and shaved his head. These were clear signs of mourning. We also see Job as he falls to the ground in worship. He speaks words of blessing and praise. Job's response is both sorrow and worship.

INTERPRETIVE INSIGHT | Does Job Fear God for Nothing?

In Job 2 we switch back to the upper stage. God says to Satan (Job 2:3):

> Have you considered my servant Job? There is no one on earth
> like him; he is blameless and upright, a man who fears God and
> shuns evil. And he still maintains his integrity, though you
> incited me against him to ruin him without any reason.

SIGNIFICANT SCRIPTURE
Job 1:6–12, 20–22

SIGNIFICANT SCRIPTURE
Job 2:1–10

Satan tells God that the only reason Job maintains his integrity is that God has treated him well. If God allowed his body to be touched with pain, he would certainly curse God.

From this point on, the action of this drama takes place on the lower stage. It is critical that we clarify what is going on in heaven. At first glance, the action in heaven looks strange and confusing. It appears as if a cosmic wager between God and Satan is taking place. It can seem as if God is using Job and his family as pawns to win a bet or prove a point to Satan.

But this is not what is going on at all. The key question on the upper stage and in the whole book is, "Does Job fear God for nothing?" Satan insists: "Job is devoted to you, God, and worships you because it's in his self-interest to do it. You scratch his back. He scratches yours. It's a quid pro quo." Satan is charging God with being naïve.

ILLUSTRATION | Why Is Job Devoted to God?

Satan, the accuser, is insisting that Job's devotion is strictly based on what he is getting from God. Satan is saying that Job loves God the way children love the ice cream man. He loves God the way a drug addict loves a drug dealer. It is all quid pro quo.

Satan is arguing that if you turn off the faucet of blessing, watch how fast Job turns off the faucet of devotion. If Job is the best man on earth and the rest are worse than him, his response will speak volumes for the human family. Satan is saying that the whole idea of a covenant of self-giving love between God and people is a farce. It's all a joke.

NARRATIVE ON LIFE | Evolutionary Biology

The reality of the universe is that everybody's looking out for number one—quid pro quo. This philosophy is extremely current. One dominant view of human nature in the secular culture of our day is called evolutionary biology. The idea is that human beings are simply gene carriers programmed to engage in whatever behavior will maximize the odds that their genes will survive. This same idea was expressed long ago.

INTERPRETIVE INSIGHT | Who Is on Trial?

The writer of Job makes masterful use of irony through this book. The ultimate irony is this: We think this is a book where God is on trial. With all the suffering

---

WORD STUDY

Quid Pro Quo

The *Webster's New Universal Unabridged Dictionary* gives this primary definition of "quid pro quo": "*Latin*. One thing in return for another." The idea of quid pro quo is that one person will do something only as a response for what he or she has received. In the book of Job, the idea is that Job is only honoring God because God has been good to him. Satan argues that once Job stops receiving things from God, he will stop honoring God.

in the world, can God be truly good? On the lower stage, that is the primary question in this book. But, we can also see the action on the upper stage. We can see that there is a God in heaven. This is really a book where the human race is on trial. Satan (the accuser) is the prosecuting attorney who is pointing a finger at us.

Satan is saying, "People are nothing more than slaves to their own self interest. The whole thing is a farce; people will only love God if he gives them what they want."

God says, "No. Satan has it all wrong!" He makes it clear that the view presented by Satan is cynical, warped, misguided, and wrong. "At the core of this universe is self-giving, self-sacrificing love. Human beings were made to receive and give that kind of love. They are capable of it, when they are experiencing pleasure, and even when they face days of pain."

NARRATIVE ON LIFE | ## Responding to Pain

After losing all his possessions and his children, Job gets hit with a second wave of suffering. His body is afflicted with pain most of us can't even imagine. This time his response is different. He does *not* fall to the ground and worship. He does *not* say, "May the name of the LORD be praised."

This time Job sits on an ash heap. Maybe he's grieving. Maybe he's isolated since people are afraid he has leprosy. His wife speaks for the first and last time in this drama. She simply says: "Are you still holding on to your integrity? Curse God and die!" (Job 2:9).

NARRATIVE ON THE TEXT | ## Meeting Mrs. Job

Mrs. Job gets criticized a lot by preachers and teachers. She seems like an easy target. Job's first response is a measured expression of sorrow and enduring worship. Her first recorded response is a suggestion that Job curse God and die. But before we judge her too harshly, we must remember what she is experiencing. Job and his wife were real people with real feelings.

She too has lost all that she had. She has lost all her children. Her husband is covered with sores and is experiencing indescribable pain. She sees him and must be wondering what it will mean to care for a horribly diseased husband until he recovers or dies. A short time ago she was part of the wealthiest family in the East. Now she and her husband are utterly alone and destitute. Before we judge her too harshly, we should ask how we might react in a similar situation.

SIGNIFICANT SCRIPTURE

Job 2:7-10

WORD STUDY

Nud

Job was famous because of his great wealth. Today he is famous because of his great suffering. We read that his friends "met . . . to . . . sympathize with him." The word for "sympathize" here is the Hebrew verb *nud*. This word means to rock back and forth. It was used to describe a specific body movement where a person rocked back and forth after a time of pain or trauma.

Sometimes when people go through a tremendous trauma and are in shock, they begin rocking. It is almost uncontrollable—automatic. They rock themselves back and forth like a mother comforting a baby. The word *nud* describes this motion of maternal comforting.

NARRATIVE ON LIFE | Struggling to Understand God

Job's response (Job 2:10) shows that he is struggling to understand God: "You are talking like a foolish woman. Shall we accept good from God, and not trouble?" The words "and not trouble" can be translated "and not evil." Job is struggling to understand if God is the kind of person who sends evil. Is God really good? That is the question on the lower stage.

Then the text says: "In all this, Job did not sin in what he said." This is a little hint of what is going on inside Job. After the first wave of suffering Job faced, we are told that "in all this, Job did not sin by charging God with wrongdoing." Now, after this second wave of suffering, there's a little qualification: "Job did not sin in what he said." Job has begun to struggle in his heart, but he is not expressing it in words—yet.

NARRATIVE ON THE TEXT | Support in a Time of Grief

Job's friends plan to sit next to him and take on his anguish. When they see Job, they can hardly recognize him. They heard it was bad, but nothing could prepare them for what they see when they meet Job.

Usually when we visit somebody who is sick or in a bad condition, we try to cheer them up. Have you ever been so sick that when someone comes to visit you, they take one look and burst into tears? That's what happens to Job. It is so awful that all they can do is weep. Then, they do something remarkable. They just sit with him for seven days and seven nights and do not say a word. They are with him in silence.

LIFE APPLICATION | Mourning Times Two

When we mourn with those who mourn and sit with those who are hurting, we are not trying to fix them. We don't come to give some clever advice that will make everything better. One of the greatest gifts we give is our presence. It is interesting to note that the silence of Job's friends was brilliant. It was a gift. Their words later became torment.

ON THE LIGHTER SIDE | An Extra Friend

Job's friends hear all about the troubles that have come on him. They want to see him and help him through this painful time. They meet together and go to find Job so they can sympathize with him and give him comfort in his time of pain. His friends are: Eliphaz the Temanite, Bildad the Shuhite, Zophar the Naamathite, Dadgum the Termite. OK, the last one, Dadgum the Termite is not in the text. That is just thrown in to make sure everyone is paying attention.

Do you have friends who would sit with you through a time of suffering? Do you have people who would sit quietly with you just for the sake of offering support? If so, give thanks to God! If not, think seriously about connecting with a small group of Christ followers who can support and comfort you.

Also, ask yourself who would be comforted by your presence if they were hurting. Do you have people you can sit with when they are in need of a friend? If not, commit to deepen your relationships and be sure to make yourself available to those who are in need.

3. The Characters Speak

NARRATIVE ON THE TEXT | Job Speaks

Finally, after seven days of silence, Job speaks. This is a remarkable thing. Imagine the tension that has built up. Seven days have passed, and his friends are still waiting to hear what Job will say. Will he repeat what he said in chapter 1: "The LORD gave and the LORD has taken away; may the name of the LORD be praised." If he could just repeat those words again, the whole test is over. This would be a tiny book.

We don't wait long before we realize that Job's words will not echo what he said in chapter 1.

> After this, Job opened his mouth and cursed the day of his birth.
> He said:
>
> "May the day of my birth perish,
>   and the night it was said, 'A boy is born!'
> That day—may it turn to darkness;
>   may God above not care about it;
>   may no light shine upon it. (Job 3:1–4)

HISTORICAL CONTEXT

Sitting Sevens

The example of Job's friends sitting with him for seven days in silence was such a powerful act that it became a part of Jewish life even to this day. In the Jewish tradition, they will speak of "sitting Shiva." Literally this means "sitting sevens." Friends will come to sit with one who mourns over a period of a week.

SIGNIFICANT SCRIPTURE

Job 2:11-15; 3

CREATIVE MESSAGE IDEA | Silence

Consider taking a short time of silence with all those who are gathered. Ask everyone to sit in silence, not to say a word. How long is it before the silence becomes uncomfortable? Is it a few seconds, a few minutes, maybe an hour? For the friends of Job, all they can do at this point is be silent and be with him—for seven entire days.

This is the kind of thing that keeps Job off the motivational speaker circuit. Things get pretty dark as he goes on to curse his birthday. Job will not curse God, but he does curse the day God made him. This seems like a sneaky way of getting at the same thing. For the rest of the book, Job pours out a level of bitterness, confusion, sorrow, and anger toward God that is staggering.

NARRATIVE ON THE TEXT | Job's Friends Speak

Job spews so much venom that his three friends can't stand it. They can't listen to it. Finally they respond—and most of the book of Job is a series of speeches given by Job and his friends' responses. We can't look at all of the speeches, but we can identify the key theme each of Job's friends brings forth.

Eliphaz argues that the innocent don't perish and the upright are not destroyed. In effect, he is saying that the innocent don't suffer.

> Consider now: Who, being innocent, has ever perished?
> Where were the upright ever destroyed? (Job 4:7)

Bildad gets a little more direct. He says that Job's children died because of their sin. They had it coming! His theory is that our suffering is a result of personal sin and rebellion.

> When your children sinned against him,
> he gave them over to the penalty of their sin. (Job 8:4)

Zophar suggests that Job's suffering is a result of his personal sin. He calls Job to repent and turn from his sin.

> Yet if you devote your heart to him
> and stretch out your hands to him,
> if you put away the sin that is in your hand
> and allow no evil to dwell in your tent,
> then you will lift up your face without shame;
> you will stand firm and without fear. (Job 11:13–15)

HISTORICAL CONTEXT | The Doctrine of Retribution

The view of Job's friends expressed in this book was the primary theology of suffering in Job's day. In Israel and the surrounding area, this was the conventional wisdom. It's written about in what scholars call the "Mesopotamian Wisdom Literature." It is sometimes called the doctrine of retribution. The idea of this theology is simple. Goodness results in prosperity and blessing, and wickedness results in suffering.

In each case, when Job's friends put forth their theory, Job counters with his argument and defense. At one point Job gets testy and somewhat sarcastic: "Doubtless you are the people, and wisdom will die with you!" (Job 12:2). It is important that we hear Job's three friends giving voice to one central idea. Their view is that pain, suffering, and sorrow in this life are a direct consequence for personal sin.

NARRATIVE ON LIFE | ## Some Things Never Change

Philip Yancey notes that the arguments voiced by Job's friends are still repeated in Christian churches today. Yancey writes that suffering people have told him that those who make their suffering worse are often well-meaning Christians who are confused about this very issue. These are some of the lines that well-intentioned but confused Christians might use:

- "The reason that you're in the hospital is spiritual warfare. If you were just standing strong and walking in the power of Jesus, Satan would be defeated. You'd be delivered."

- "God promises to heal if we have enough faith. If you will pray with enough faith, you will be healed." (Implication—if you're not healed, you're not praying with enough faith.)

- "God has handpicked you to suffer to bring him greater glory. You just need to thank him for the pain you're suffering, because it's glorifying him."

- "Your suffering is a wake-up call. It's a punishment for sin. You need to figure out what you've done wrong and repent."

LIFE APPLICATION | ## Sincere, But Sincerely Wrong

This doctrine of retribution goes all the way back to the book of Job. It's that old. Eliphaz, one of Job's friends, even claims he has divine insight. He says, "A word was secretly brought to me, my ears caught a whisper of it" (Job 4:12). We need to be careful about telling people that God has given us a word of knowledge for them. Eliphaz is sincere, but he's wrong. He did not speak a word from God for Job. Before we speak such a word or receive such a word, we had better be sure it is really from God.

INTERPRETIVE INSIGHT | The Implications

The doctrine of retribution inevitably turns God into a means for pursuing good circumstances—the blessed life. Pretty soon we are not trying to pursue God. Rather, we are trying to use God. When Christians buy into this system of belief, they become smug, self-righteous, and judgmental when things are going well. When things are going badly, they fall into despair. This is why God teaches us that this way of seeing things is absolutely wrong!

NARRATIVE ON LIFE | The Value of True Friends

Job suffers under the judgmental words of his friends. Along the way he responds with these words:

> A despairing man should have the devotion of his friends,
> even though he forsakes the fear of the Almighty.
> (Job 6:14)

Right in the midst of a battle of words, Job makes this remarkable statement about friendship. In other words, a real friend doesn't give up on you no matter what; even when it looks like your faith is on the ash heap.

NARRATIVE ON LIFE | All Over the Map

SIGNIFICANT SCRIPTURE

Job 19

People in anguish often contradict themselves. They seem to move all over the emotional map. In Job 19 Job goes through all kinds of emotions. Everything he feels and says does not make sense, but he pours it all out. What a great reminder for us that God knows all that is inside us and he allows us to express it honestly.

NARRATIVE ON THE TEXT | Taking God to Court

SIGNIFICANT SCRIPTURE

Job 23:1–10

As Job goes on, he questions God, he clings to God, he hollers at God, and he hollers for God. Mostly, he challenges God. Job's boldness is staggering:

> If only I knew where to find him;
> if only I could go to his dwelling!
> I would state my case before him
> and fill my mouth with arguments. (Job 23:3–4)

It is as if Job wants to take God to court. He wants to sue him. Job is challenging God to show up so they can fight man to man.

NARRATIVE ON THE TEXT | God Speaks

SIGNIFICANT SCRIPTURE

Job 38–41

In chapter 38, Job gets his wish. God answers Job out of the storm! What do you think that moment was like? Do you think there was a little drama? Do you think the atmosphere changed when God showed up in a storm?

God says, "OK, Job, let's have a face off!" Then, for the next four chapters, God speaks! Job and his friends remain quiet. God has now come from the upper stage to the lower stage. Moreover, he has some questions for Job! Over and over God asks Job about how the creation came into being. He asks him about specific animals. He puts Job on the witness stand, but Job has little to say!

INTERPRETIVE INSIGHT | A Finite Mind

Part of what's happening is that God is reminding Job that he has a finite mind and a limited point of view. Only God can see the whole story. An Old Testament scholar by the name of Ellen Davis notices that God's questions actually give great insight into the kind of person he is. He is the kind of God who creates in such a way that the morning stars sing together and the angels shout for joy! In this portion of Job, God's creative beauty shines through, and his delight in creation is clear to see.

INTERPRETIVE INSIGHT | God Delights in His Creation

All through this section we see God delighting in his creation. Even creatures that are of no apparent and no strategic value are a joy to God. There is no quid pro quo about it. God doesn't get anything from them, but he still loves them. A quick survey will make this very clear.

- *The ostrich* (Job 39:13–18): This is just a wonderful, fun passage. The ostrich is a goofy-looking animal. God says that she flaps her wings joyfully—as if she thinks that's going to get her somewhere. She's not a great mom. She lays her eggs but can't even remember where she left them.

- *The hippo* (40:15–19): In the ancient world, the behemoth was considered what they called the chaos monster. Some people wrote that it had to be eliminated for the earth to be habitable for human beings. But that's not God's opinion. God ranks this strange creature as a great success among his works of God.

- *The wild ox, the donkey,* and other animals are listed. You can't miss God's joy and celebration of his creation.

The Creator loves pizzazz. He revels in the beauty and delight and joy of the least strategic creature that will never do him any good. He just loves to give.

—ANNIE DILLARD

LIFE APPLICATION | So Should We!

If God delights in his creation, so should we. We need to slow down and look around us. There are colorful birds, strange insects, and animals all over the place. The stars shine, the oceans crash, and the trees lift their hands. We need to be like God in our appreciation of his wondrous creative work. It is time for us to notice and celebrate.

ILLUSTRATION | The Creator Loves His World

Why would God make and love a world like ours? Annie Dillard writes: "Because the Creator loves pizzazz. Because he revels in the beauty and delight and joy of the least strategic creature that will never do him any good. He just loves to give."

The God of the upper stage is a God who is endlessly good, uncontrollably generous, and irrationally loving! He gives no reason for this, nor does he have to! It is his nature.

NARRATIVE ON THE TEXT | I Can Trust You!

By the end of the story, Job finds out the kind of person God is, and that's enough for him. The hinge—the resolution of this whole book—is in 42:5–6. Job is speaking to God:

> My ears had heard of you
>   but now my eyes have seen you.
> Therefore I despise myself
>   and repent in dust and ashes.

This is enough for Job. He has heard, he has seen, he is satisfied! When Job says that he repents in dust and ashes, he is not saying, "I will now live with low self-esteem." This is a Hebrew way of saying he is entering into a new strategy for living. He is saying to God, "I can trust you." We can almost hear Job declare, "I can trust you with my children; I know that they are better off in your hands now. I can trust you with my pain; I know that you will redeem every bit of it. You are the kind of God who treasures and cares for everything. I place my full trust in you."

4. The Epilogue

The book of Job ends with restoration and blessing (Job 42:12–17):

**SIGNIFICANT
SCRIPTURE**

Job 42:12-17

> The LORD blessed the latter part of Job's life more than the first. He had fourteen thousand sheep, six thousand camels, a thousand yoke of oxen and a thousand donkeys. And he also had seven sons and three daughters. The first daughter he named Jemimah, the second Keziah and the third Keren-Happuch. Nowhere in all the land were there found women as beautiful as Job's daughters, and their father granted them an inheritance along with their brothers.
>
> After this, Job lived a hundred and forty years; he saw his children and their children to the fourth generation. And so he died, old and full of years.

INTERPRETIVE INSIGHT | The Truth about God and Us

Why does the writer include all these strange details? It seems these things are there to reflect what is happening in the heart of Job. He is now delighting in those who are seen as the least strategic of creatures. Job is becoming gratuitously good, uncontrollably generous, and irrationally loving. In short, he is being shaped into the image of the God he has met and learned to trust.

Satan was dead wrong about Job. He was also wrong about the human race. He was wrong about the universe. And he was dead wrong about God. The book of Job is *not* about some odd, cosmic wager. It was written so you and I could know what the truth is about us and God.

HISTORICAL CONTEXT | Blessing the Daughters

There are some details in Job 42:12-17 that we might miss, but they would have jumped out at ancient readers. In the first place, the writer gives us the names of Job's daughters but not of his sons. This was unheard of in ancient Hebrew genealogies. This was unprecedented because the sons were the ones, in the ancient world, whose names got mentioned.

Usually, Hebrew names are serious, especially the ones that make it into the Bible. They express character, virtue, or theological truth. The three names given for Job's daughters are all about the beauty of creation.

· *Jemimah* is the name for a dove—a bird that was prized for its beauty.
· *Keziah* means cinnamon. It was a prized spice.

· *Keren-Happuch* was the oddest one. It means "horn of eye shadow." She was named after make-up. This would be like naming your daughter Estee Lauder or Maybelline.

Not only did Job give them strange names, he also gave them an inheritance. In an ancient, male-dominated world, a father with seven sons would never dream of leaving something to a daughter.

PAUSE FOR PRAYER

Give a short time for prayer, both silent and out loud. Then, close the time with a prayer for each person who is living in the land of Uz to meet God in a new and powerful way. Pray for strength for them to make it through. Pray that God will bring friends alongside of them who will sit with them, love them, and see them through.

NARRATIVE ON LIFE | A Word to Those Living in Uz

Job never got to look on the upper stage. He never realized that his faithfulness had meaning beyond his own life. He did not know that something cosmic and eternal was at stake in his little life. When he was sitting on an ash heap, scraping boils off his skin with shards of broken pots, he did not know what was happening on the upper stage. Even though he was broken, sick, mocked, confused, and hopeless, Job's faithfulness was used by God to vindicate God's whole wild adventure in covenant love.

Job's honesty, courage, tenacity, and perseverance have inspired billions of people who have lived in the land of Uz. Job still speaks out and says, "Hang on. Keep going. Don't let go. Don't give up. Don't quit now."

LIFE APPLICATION | Living in the Land of Uz

Some of those gathered and hearing this message are in a time of pain, sorrow, and suffering. This is the land of Uz.

> Why are you there? I don't know.
>
> How long will it last? I don't know.
>
> Does your response matter? Does what you do and how you live make any difference at all? More than you could ever dream.

The eyes of heaven are on our little lives as we travel through the land of Uz. What we do is of eternal and cosmic significance to God.

CREATIVE MESSAGE IDEA | Offering Support

Invite those gathered to take a moment and ask a person sitting near them how they can support them in prayer. Allow a time for people to talk. Then, encourage people to pray together. They can do this out loud or silently. This is not a time to give answers to each other or try to solve problems. It is a time to pray for God's comfort, presence, and love to flow into the lives of all those who are living in the land of Uz.

The Divided Kingdom: What Puts Community at Risk?

1 KINGS 12–15

The Heart of the
MESSAGE

First Kings 12–15 is one of the saddest sections in the Old Testament. What began as the magic kingdom under David became the tragic kingdom under David's successors. What started out as Camelot under Solomon deteriorated into civil war and chaos upon Solomon's death. The unity and community that had been experienced for over a hundred years was soon to be shattered by civil war!

In this session we will be learning from the demise of the community of ancient Israel. We will look at their mistakes so that we can avoid taking those same paths. One of the reasons we study the Old Testament is to learn from the past so that we will not repeat the same mistakes and enter into the same folly. Historians tell us that those who do not remember the past are condemned to repeat it. Thus, in this session we want to discover those factors that contributed to the downfall of the community of ancient Israel so that we can discover what puts biblical community at risk. Once these things have been identified, we can seek to avoid them and build a biblically functioning community that is marked by an enduring spirit of unity.

The Heart of the
MESSENGER

In this session we will identify four factors that put community at risk. Take time before you teach this session to examine your heart and life. Do any of these community-breaking patterns exist in your life? Do you need to change a life pattern or attitude for the sake of becoming more of a community builder? Take time to ask God to shape you into a follower of Christ who blesses and builds community.

Brief Message
OUTLINE

1. Understanding the Times

2. Risk Factor 1: Failing to Be a Servant Leader

3. Risk Factor 2: Using Spiritual Language for Selfish Motives

4. Risk Factor 3: Following God Halfheartedly

5. Risk Factor 4: Turning Away from God

1. Understanding the Times

All We Need to Know

As you read through the history of Israel, you will discover that events are not always recorded chronologically. Some people get concerned about this. In modern history books, we tend to list things in a clear chronology. The Bible is historically reliable. But we must remember that it is not primarily given as a history book. It has not been given to us to satisfy our historical curiosities. The Bible is primarily given to us to reveal the character of God, to change our lives, and to help us become the people he wants us to be. The Bible does not always tell us everything we want to know. However, it does tell us everything we need to know for building a living relationship with God and for developing community with other people.

The Measure of a King

As we study the books of Kings and Chronicles, we are introduced to thirty-nine kings of Israel and Judah. This message focuses on the Divided Kingdom Period. There is a formula that's followed for almost every one of the kings from both the north and south. It goes like this: Each king is introduced by stating the length of his reign. His reign is then synchronized with the reign of the corresponding king in the other kingdom. Each king is compared to his immediate predecessor as

---

A Basic Timeline

Before we look at the community risk factors, we should look at some introductory information about this section of the Bible. It's important, first of all, to understand that the kingdom period of ancient Israel lasted about five hundred years—from 1050 to 586 B.C. This period of history can be broken into four distinct phases.

(1) The first phase was the *United Kingdom Period* under Kings Saul, David, and Solomon. This lasted 120 years.

(2) Next was the *Divided Kingdom Period*. This is when civil war broke out between Israel and Judah. During this time, ten tribes of Israel formed the northern kingdom with Samaria as its capital and Jeroboam as its king. The two tribes of Judah and Benjamin formed the southern kingdom with Jerusalem as its capital and Rehoboam as its king. This phase lasted about two hundred years.

(3) In 722 B.C. the northern kingdom (Israel) was attacked, destroyed, and dispersed to the four corners of the ancient world. This marked the beginning of phase three—the *Surviving Kingdom Period* of the south (Judah). For about 136 years Judah survived, but then the Babylonians came and invaded. They destroyed Jerusalem and took many of the people to Babylonia as exiles for seventy years.

(4) This exile marks the fourth phase of the kingdom: the *Dissolved Kingdom Period*. Israel, the northern kingdom, had been gone for generations. Now Judah, the southern kingdom, was exiled to a foreign land. They were prisoners of war. At this point, the kingdom was dissolved. Although a remnant came back to the land under the leadership of Zerubbabel and later Ezra and Nehemiah, the history of God's people as a nation with a human king from their midst was over.

either being better or worse. And all of the kings are evaluated against the benchmark of King David as either being good or evil in comparison to him. We see this formula, for example, in 1 Kings 15:1–3:

> In the eighteenth year of the reign of Jeroboam son of Nebat, Abijah became king of Judah, and he reigned in Jerusalem three years. His mother's name was Maacah daughter of Abishalom.
>
> He committed all the sins his father had done before him; his heart was not fully devoted to the LORD his God, as the heart of David his forefather had been.

NARRATIVE ON LIFE | How God Sees Us

We tend to evaluate greatness by a leader's achievements, but God evaluates greatness by a person's character. In the life of every one of the kings of Israel and Judah a simple and divine evaluation is given. God declares an epitaph for each one. He either says, "He was good," or "He was evil." Of the twenty kings of Israel, all of them "did evil" in God's sight. Only eight of the kings of Judah "did good." The truth is that even kings and presidents answer to a higher authority. They may think they are sovereign and the last word, but they are not. And neither are we! We should all ask the question: "What will God say about my life when it's all over?"

2. Risk Factor 1: Failing to Be a Servant Leader

The rest of this message will focus on four community risk factors we find in the books of Kings and Chronicles. God wants unity and health in the community of his followers, but often this is not the reality we experience. By learning from

ON THE LIGHTER SIDE | A Look at Presidents

Most nations and cultures evaluate their leaders in some way. In the United States most people have an idea of who they think is the greatest president ever. Invite those gathered to lean over to the person next to them and say who they think was voted as the best president ever.

According to an ABC news poll conducted on Presidents Day weekend every year, the largest group of people said Abraham Lincoln was the greatest president in U.S. history. In 2002, this poll showed the top three presidents as: Abraham Lincoln, John F. Kennedy, and George W. Bush.

some of the mistakes made in the time of the kings, we can discover how to build community and avoid the pitfalls they experienced.

Nothing puts community at risk more than a leader who takes advantage of people for selfish gain. Those who never learn the principle of being a servant leader will watch the erosion of community all around them. By contrast, when a leader uses his or her position and power to serve others, this generates loyalty and strengthens community.

NARRATIVE ON THE TEXT | Lighten the Load!

SIGNIFICANT SCRIPTURE

1 Kings 12:1-17

One of the defining moments for the community of ancient Israel came when Rehoboam succeeded Solomon, his father, as king. At his inauguration, when the leaders of the twelve tribes of Israel came to crown their new king, he had an opportunity to build community—to strengthen community—and instead he blew it up.

The elders of the twelve tribes came with one request to Rehoboam: "Your father put a heavy yoke on us, but now lighten the harsh labor and the heavy yoke he put on us, and we will serve you" (1 Kings 12:4). Rehoboam responded by asking for three days to think about it.

During those days he sought counsel from the elders who had served his father, Solomon. Here is what they said: "If today you will be a servant to these people and serve them and give them a favorable answer, they will always be your servants" (1 Kings 12:7).

Then Rehoboam consulted the young men he had grown up with. Their advice was different (see 1 Kings 12:10–11):

> "Tell these people who have said to you, 'Your father put a heavy yoke on us, but make our yoke lighter'—tell them, 'My little finger is thicker than my father's waist. My father laid on you a heavy yoke; I will make it even heavier. My father scourged you with whips; I will scourge you with scorpions.'"

HISTORICAL CONTEXT | The Twelve Tribes

When we talk about the division of the kingdom and the fracturing of the twelve tribes of Israel, we need to remember their history. These were the descendants of Abraham, Isaac, and Jacob, the great patriarchs of Israel. Jacob had twelve sons, who became the heads of the tribes of Israel. These tribes were all family. Many years and generations had passed, but the tribes of Israel who were part of the united kingdom were all related to each other. When this division came and civil war ensued, this was a division of God's covenantal people—and blood relatives.

After listening to both sides of advice, Rehoboam refused the path of service. Instead, he decided to rule with an iron fist, and it cost him the unity of the kingdom. Over a century of the twelve tribes being united ended when Rehoboam declared that he would not be a servant leader.

NARRATIVE ON THE TEXT | A Divided Kingdom

How do you think the people responded to Rehoboam's decision to reject the path of being a servant to the people? How do you think they reacted to his declaration that their load would be even heavier and that he would be scourging them with scorpions?

The answer is, they responded very predictably. They cried out:

> When all Israel saw that the king refused to listen to them, they answered the king:
>
> "What share do we have in David,
>   what part in Jesse's son?
> To your tents, O Israel!
>   Look after your own house, O David!" (1 Kings 12:16)

In other words, they said, "Forget you! We don't need you. We'll choose our own king." And that's exactly what they did. They appointed Jeroboam as king over the ten tribes of the north and set his throne in Samaria. Rehoboam's foolish, self-serving decision caused the people to rebel, and it divided the kingdom and birthed a civil war that lasted for over two centuries.

NARRATIVE ON LIFE | Defining Moments

Rehoboam failed to be a servant leader. He abused his position. He did not listen to wise counsel. He was more concerned about himself than his people, and he put the community of Israel into a tailspin from which they never recovered. It was a defining moment in his life and in the history of Israel.

In the same way, leaders today consign their churches, businesses, families, and any group of people to disunity when they refuse to be servant leaders. Every leader faces the same defining moment Rehoboam encountered. *Will I serve or demand that I be served? Will I build community or destroy it?*

LIFE APPLICATION | An A-WICS Attitude

At a church in Grand Rapids, Michigan, the staff members talk about having an A-WICS attitude. This came from one staff member who was often heard saying, "Any way I can serve!" Over and over as opportunities to serve presented

---

NEW TESTAMENT CONNECTION

The Greatest Example

In all of history, the greatest example of a servant leader is Jesus Christ. To the surprise of his followers, Jesus Christ, the Son of God, declared that he came as a servant. His words are as staggering today as they were when he first said, "For even the Son of Man did not come to be served, but to serve, and to give his life as a ransom for many" (Mark 10:45).

Later, before he went to the cross, Jesus again affirmed his commitment to live as a servant. He washed the feet of his followers. This was one of the most humble and menial tasks a servant could do in those days. After he offered this profound act of servant leadership, he said:

> "Do you understand what I have done for you? . . . You call me 'Teacher' and 'Lord,' and rightly so, for that is what I am. Now that I, your Lord and Teacher, have washed your feet, you also should wash one another's feet. I have set you an example that you should do as I have done for you. I tell you the truth, no servant is greater than his master, nor is a messenger greater than the one who sent him. Now that you know these things, you will be blessed if you do them." (John 13:12–17)

PAUSE FOR PRAYER

Make Me a Servant

You may want to pause and pray for all those gathered to grow a heart that longs to serve. Pray for humility and for an expanding understanding of how Jesus has served us as well as how he calls us to serve each other.

Your attitude should be the same as that of Christ Jesus:

Who, being in very nature God,
did not consider equality
with God something to
be grasped,
but made himself nothing,
taking the very nature of
a servant,
being made in human
likeness.
And being found in appearance
as a man,
he humbled himself
and became obedient to
death—even death on a
cross!
Therefore God exalted him to
the highest place
and gave him the name that
is above every name,
that at the name of Jesus every
knee should bow,
in heaven and on earth and
under the earth,
and every tongue confess that
Jesus Christ is Lord,
to the glory of God the
Father.

—*The apostle Paul in*
Philippians 2:6–11

themselves, she kept saying, "Any way I can serve." Even when a task or project was not in her area of ministry or under her job description, she kept looking for ways to serve and support others.

At some point along the way, the pastor coined the phrase, "An A-WICS Attitude." This term describes a person who is ready to say:

Any **W**ay **I C**an **S**erve!

Consider adopting an A-WICS attitude in your home, church, workplace, and wherever else God leads you. You MAY even want to write this word somewhere you will see it on a regular basis as a reminder of Jesus' call for us to serve each other. If someone sees it and asks you what it means, let them know how you have been served by Jesus and how you are called to a life of serving others.

3. Risk Factor 2: Using Spiritual Language for Selfish Motives

Community is at risk when people seek to manipulate others by using spiritual language to accomplish selfish purposes. This happened in the days of the kings, and it still happens today. Every time someone seeks to leverage another person with hyperspiritual language, we need to be cautious and make sure we know their motives.

NARRATIVE ON THE TEXT | Don't Strain Yourselves

Although the kingdom was divided politically, with Rehoboam as the king in the south and Jeroboam as the king in the north, they were still united spiritually. All of the Israelites in both kingdoms were still expected to make a pilgrimage several times a year to Jerusalem to worship God. Jerusalem was still the location of the temple and the center of the religious life of all Israelites. It also happened to be the capital of the southern kingdom and the place where Rehoboam ruled! This caused a problem for Jeroboam, the king of Israel. He articulated his concern in 1 Kings 12:26–27:

> Jeroboam thought to himself, "The kingdom will now likely revert to the house of David. If these people go up to offer sacrifices at the temple of the LORD in Jerusalem, they will again give their allegiance to their lord, Rehoboam king of Judah. They will kill me and return to King Rehoboam."

Jeroboam was filled with fear because he knew his kingship would always be in jeopardy as long as the people under his rule went to the capital of the southern kingdom to worship. Thus, he came up with a solution. He made two golden calves and set up his own places of worship. Jeroboam established a formal system of idolatry, which was clearly forbidden! Then, in an effort to sway the people of Israel away from Jerusalem and toward his new places of worship, he said: "It is too much for you to go up to Jerusalem. Here are your gods, O Israel, who brought you up out of Egypt" (1 Kings 12:28).

Nothing can get a biblically functioning community going down the wrong path faster than individuals who manipulate spiritual language for personal agendas. That was the sin of Jeroboam. He made idols for his own political agenda, and then he manipulated people into following his false gods. We must be careful when people use spiritual language in dogmatic tones. It could put a community at risk.

NARRATIVE ON LIFE | "God Told Me!"

There is a word for people who do what Jeroboam did: *manipulation!* Community is at risk when people use spiritual language for selfish motives. Jeroboam manipulated people by using religious language for his personal, political agenda. Clearly he was not concerned about the people truly worshiping God. He just wanted to be sure their hearts did not turn back to Jerusalem and the king who ruled there.

This still happens in churches today. When people use God-talk in dogmatic terms and in demanding tones so that they can get what they want, that's spiritual manipulation. Every time someone uses spiritual language to advance his or her personal agenda, it is a recipe for broken community. We must learn to have our antennas up so that we can identify when this is happening—specifically, when people come to us saying things like:

- "God spoke to me and told me you should . . ."

- "God told me his plan for you is . . ."

- "God showed me that our church has to . . ."

- "Pastor, I have a word for you from God! He said . . ."

We must approach this topic with a double caution. First, let's admit that God does speak and we must listen when others have received a word from God. We must take care not to miss when God is speaking to us or his church. Yet the second caution, and one that applies to the passage we are studying, is that we must be careful when people are using spiritual language to forward their own selfish agendas. This happened in Jeroboam's day, and it still happens today.

SIGNIFICANT SCRIPTURE

1 Kings 12:25–33

ILLUSTRATION | "I Was Wrong!"

If you have your own story of someone who used spiritual language to manipulate you or someone you know, you may want to use it at this time. You can also use the story Jim Tomberlin told in his message.

A pastor tells of how he now lives with a real sensitivity to the issue of spiritual language being used to manipulate someone. You see, he was a victim! When Jim was a college student, he was a young and naïve Christian. He got involved with a Christian organization on campus. In that organization was a really cute girl who caught his eye. To his joyful surprise, it seemed he caught her eye as well!

One day she came up to Jim and said, "God told me you're the one." He thought to himself, "Who am I to question God? If God told her I am the one, how can I argue with that?" He was smitten. He was head over heels in love—or maybe infatuation, but it felt like love.

Three months later, she dumped Jim, and it broke his heart.

Jim asked her, "What happened? I thought God spoke to you and told you I was the one." Her answer staggered him: "I was wrong."

Jim learned a lesson that day that we would all be wise to learn. Whenever someone uses superspiritual language, has a dogmatic tone, and is insistent that they know God's will for you and everyone else, it is wise to be cautious! This does not mean that we refuse to let God speak to us through others. What it does mean is that we need to use discernment and wisdom and to take great care with those who are quick to declare God's will for our lives.

LIFE APPLICATION | Be Careful

God still speaks! There is no question about this. However, we must live with two cautions that will prove helpful in our effort to become the people God wants us to be. (1) We must be wise in how we listen to others. When you bump into people who are emphatic and dogmatic about knowing God's will for your life, be cautious. You should seek the wisdom of the Holy Spirit and godly counsel from people you trust. In other words, if someone comes up to you and says, "God told me you are the one!" you had better be sure he or she did in fact hear it from God before you dive into the relationship.

(2) You must also be careful that you are not guilty of using spiritual language to manipulate others. If you have gotten into the habit of declaring what God wants others to do, you should humbly look at your motives. If God is giving you divine promptings that will help others, great! You can humbly share what is on your heart and let God move people as he will. But, if you tend to be

PAUSE FOR REFLECTION

Heart Check

Take time for personal reflection. Invite those gathered to quietly reflect on their own lives. Encourage them to identify if they are being manipulated or if they are manipulating others with spiritual language. Give time for each person to identify if community is being broken because of a misuse of spiritual language.

dogmatic and demanding, if your language is heavily spiritualized, and if you sense you may be seeking to manipulate people, it is time to stop. This is sin—and God wants us to repent!

4. Risk Factor 3: Following God Halfheartedly

God calls us to be fully devoted followers. He wants 100 percent from us. When we follow him with a halfhearted devotion, we will see community erode all around us. This is a huge risk factor!

SIGNIFICANT
SCRIPTURE

1 Kings 15:1-3

NARRATIVE ON THE TEXT | A Heart Not Fully Devoted

Abijah became the king of Judah after Rehoboam. When we read of his life and how God evaluated him, we are struck by these words: "He committed all the sins his father had done before him; his heart was not fully devoted to the LORD his God, as the heart of David his forefather had been" (1 Kings 15:3).

The sin of halfheartedness repeats itself over and over again during the history of the kings. Abijah was a king who did not follow God with his whole heart. He soon discovered that following God halfheartedly is not only foolish; it's dangerous. The problem with a heart that is only half full of God is that it is half empty! This leaves room for other affections to move in and crowd God out. It opens the door for idolatry, which is exactly what crept into Abijah's heart, just as it had entered the heart of his father. When our hearts are only half full of God, we become vulnerable to temptation, sin, and all kinds of evil. A heart that is not fully devoted to God quickly becomes a heart that wanders away.

NARRATIVE ON LIFE | Two Kinds of People

There are really two kinds of Christians when it comes to the matter of devotion. (1) There are those Christians who are fully devoted followers of Christ. These are people who live with a deep level of surrender and commitment before God. When God leads, they follow. They understand that their whole life is under the lordship of Jesus Christ, not just a few selected areas they want to devote.

(2) There are those who are half-devoted Christians. They give God some of their heart, some obedience, and some devotion. They want God, but they also want to cling to the things of the world. These people are half full of God, but they are also filled with all kinds of things that poison their heart and destroy the community God longs to build.

NEW TESTAMENT CONNECTION

Taking up the Cross

Jesus was clear that he called his followers to full devotion. He said:

> If anyone would come after me, he must deny himself and take up his cross and follow me. For whoever wants to save his life will lose it, but whoever loses his life for me will find it. (Matthew 16:24–25)

The cross is a sign of absolute surrender. To take up one's cross is to lay down one's life. This is the pathway of the fully devoted follower of Christ.

ILLUSTRATION | ## Dogs and Cats

Again, you can insert your own cat and dog story, or you can use the one below. This is not meant to exalt dogs over cats; it is simply an observation of how these two animals are wired differently.

A man tells his story of his initiation into the world of cats and dogs. This is his story:

> Several years ago my wife's parents came for a visit. On the way over they found a half-dead kitten on the side of the road. It was a cute, black-and-white kitten on the edge of death. They brought it to us, and we nursed it back to health.
>
> But when that little kitten was back to full strength, was it grateful? No! When we called its name, did it come? No! When it saw us, did it wag its tail and show that it was happy to see us? No! All we were to that cat was food and shelter. We could see that it had divided affections. It cared little about us and a lot about many other things.

The same man tells about another animal experience. He says:

> Several years ago, I brought home a twelve-week-old Golden Lab puppy. That puppy, when it was full-grown, was as devoted as you can imagine. When we called her name, she came running. When she saw us, she smiled and wagged her tail. She stayed at our feet everywhere we went. Sometimes she would wander off, but when we disciplined her, it was clear that even then, her devotion never wavered. There's a reason why dogs are man's best friend.

LIFE APPLICATION | ## Growing in Devotion

What kind of Christian are you—fully devoted or halfhearted? The amazing thing is that just as it's the nature of a dog to be loyal and devoted to its master, fully devoted followers are tenaciously committed to the master of their souls. Moreover, it is also in the nature of God to love us with unwavering passion. He longs to be our best friend.

We need to look intensely into our own hearts and see if we are fully devoted to God. If we have divided attentions, we need to set aside those things that are taking us away from full devotion and intimacy with God. Maybe we have not made time in our daily schedule to meet with our Savior. We should be sure that he gets prime time in our day. This is not some legalistic process of setting aside a mandatory devotional time. It should be the longing of our heart to be with the one who loves us so deeply. God wants us to desire to be with him and look forward to the time we can pull aside and sit at his feet, building relationship and growing in love with him.

5. Risk Factor 4: Turning Away from God

A fourth factor that puts community at risk is to turn our hearts away from God. Sometimes a follower of God does not understand something that happens in his or her life and lets his or her heart become cold toward God. Every time we turn from God, we open the door for conflict and division in community.

NARRATIVE ON THE TEXT | ### Starting Well and Finishing Poorly

Asa, one of the kings of Judah, ruled for forty-one years. He started out well. In 1 Kings 15:11 we read, "Asa did what was right in the eyes of the LORD, as his father David had done." When a superior army from Ethiopia came and invaded Judah, he called on God for help. God answered his prayer and gave him a great victory against overwhelming odds.

For thirty-five years, Asa trusted and relied on God, and he experienced peace on his borders. But there was no peace within the divided kingdom because Asa and Baasha (king of Israel) were at war throughout their reigns.

Then something happened in the thirty-sixth year of Asa's reign. The king of Israel took one of the border towns between Israel and Judah. When this happened, Asa stopped trusting in God. He turned away from God. Instead of relying on God to overcome his enemies, Asa turned to Ben-Hadad, king of Aram, for assistance. He actually robbed the gold and silver from the treasury of the temple in Jerusalem to pay this pagan king to help protect him against his own kinsmen.

Then, when a prophet came and rebuked him for turning away from God and for making an unholy alliance with a foreign king, Asa responded in anger. The Bible says he was so enraged that he put the prophet in prison and brutally

The cross is laid on every Christian. The first Christ-suffering which every man must experience is the call to abandon the attachments of this world. . . . We surrender ourselves to Christ in union with His death— we give over our lives to death. . . . When Christ calls a man, He bids him come and die.

—DIETRICH BONHOEFFER

SIGNIFICANT SCRIPTURE

1 Kings 15:9–24

PAUSE FOR PRAYER | ### With All My Heart!

One of the most amazing verses in all the Bible is found in 2 Chronicles 16:9: "For the eyes of the LORD range throughout the earth to strengthen those whose hearts are fully committed to him." God is searching all across the world, looking into the hearts of each one of us. What does he see? A heart full of God or a heart half full? He strengthens those whose hearts are fully devoted, fully committed to him.

What keeps a community of Christ followers strong? People whose hearts are fully devoted. God strengthens those people. God strengthens that congregation. Following God with half a heart puts community and individuals at great risk.

oppressed some of the people. Asa's heart had departed so far from God that he would not hear or receive godly counsel. Within a couple years, Asa died a broken and defeated man. Even in his illness he did not seek help from the Lord.

NARRATIVE ON LIFE | Could It Happen to Me?

What happened to Asa? What caused his heart to change? For so many years he had followed the path God set before him and had made many wise decisions. Then, he stopped trusting God and began placing his trust in his own wisdom and ability to figure things out.

That's a dangerous thing to do. We must realize that we are not exempt from such a change in life's direction. Maybe you even have to admit that Asa's story is your story. Maybe, like Asa, you went through a time in your life when you knew God's presence and power. You saw God work mightily in and through you. You trusted him and things happened—supernatural things, dramatic things—and you knew God was at work in your life.

Then, something changed. You faced a hard time, suffered an intense loss, made an unwise choice, or fell into a pattern of sin. Whatever happened, you slowly discovered that your heart had turned away from the God you used to love so intensely. Perhaps this is where you are today.

LIFE APPLICATION | Guarding Our Path

If something has gotten between you and God, it is time to deal with it. If you are no longer trusting in him, it is time for a change. If you have turned away from him, let this be the day you turn back. Let this be the day you say, "I will not end up like Asa. I want to be strong to the end!"

It may be helpful to reflect on the words of Proverbs 3:5–8:

> Trust in the LORD with all your heart
>   and lean not on your own understanding;
> in all your ways acknowledge him,
>   and he will make your paths straight.
> Do not be wise in your own eyes;
>   fear the LORD and shun evil.
> This will bring health to your body
>   and nourishment to your bones.

If you identify ways you are placing your trust in yourself and not in God, it is time for a change. Ask God for forgiveness. Then, place your trust in his power and wisdom, not your own.

Each of us needs to carefully examine our attitudes and actions in the days to come. Do we build community or tear it down? Are we living lives that strengthen the congregation we are part of or tear it apart? We need to learn to pray:

> Search me, O God, and know my heart;
>> test me and know my anxious thoughts.
> See if there is any offensive way in me,
>> and lead me in the way everlasting. (Psalm 139:23–24)

ILLUSTRATION | A Lesson from Lincoln

Abraham Lincoln is a dramatic contrast to Asa. Lincoln was president in the United States of America during a time of national crisis. The nation was divided. More Americans died during the Civil War than all the Americans in all the other wars. It was a time that would test the faith of any leader.

But, during that time, Lincoln relied on God. He also led the nation to rely on God. He wrote: "I have been driven, many times, to my knees by the overwhelming conviction that I had nowhere else to go."

He was a great leader. As the Civil War was coming to an end and it was clear that the North would be victorious, Lincoln was reelected for a second term as President. He delivered his second inaugural address in March of 1865.

Many of the scholars think it was his greatest speech. Sadly, it was his last speech. A month later, he was assassinated. If we read his last speech closely, we see words of healing, reconciliation, and trust in God. He concluded his speech with these words:

> With malice toward none; with charity for all; with firmness in
> the right, as God gives us to see the right, let us strive on to
> finish the work we are in; to bind up the nation's wounds; to care
> for him who shall have borne the battle, and for his widow, and
> his orphan—to do all which may achieve and cherish a just and
> lasting peace, among ourselves, and with all nations.

What a great leader! Many said that Abraham Lincoln was the best friend the South ever had. Unfortunately, he didn't live long enough to bring about the healing that needed to come to the country at that time.

NEW TESTAMENT CONNECTION

Learning from the Past

In this message we have focused on four factors that put community at risk. Each of these contributed to the demise and downfall of the community of Israel. We need to remember that God records these events in the history of Israel to serve as examples for us. In 1 Corinthians 10:11 the apostle Paul assures us that "these things happened to them as examples and were written down as warnings for us, on whom the fulfillment of the ages has come." May God give us all the wisdom to learn from these examples.

Willow Creek Association
Vision, Training, Resources for Prevailing Churches

This resource was created to serve you and to help you in building a local church that prevails!

Since 1992, the Willow Creek Association (WCA) has been linking like-minded, action-oriented churches with each other and with strategic vision, training, and resources. Now a worldwide network of over 6,400 churches from more than ninety denominations, the WCA works to equip Member Churches and others with the tools needed to build prevailing churches. Our desire is to inspire, equip, and encourage Christian leaders to build biblically functioning churches that reach increasing numbers of unchurched people, not just with innovations from Willow Creek Community Church in South Barrington, Illinois, but from any church in the world that has experienced God-given breakthroughs.

WILLOW CREEK CONFERENCES

Each year, thousands of local church leaders, staff and volunteers—from WCA Member Churches and others—attend one of our conferences or training events. Conferences offered on the Willow Creek campus in South Barrington, Illinois, include:

Prevailing Church Conference: Foundational training for staff and volunteers working to build a prevailing local church.

Prevailing Church Workshops: More than fifty strategic, day-long workshops covering seven topic areas that represent key characteristics of a prevailing church; offered twice each year.

Promiseland Conference: Children's ministries; infant through fifth grade.

Student Ministries Conference: Junior and senior high ministries.

Willow Creek Arts Conference: Vision and training for Christian artists using their gifts in the ministries of local churches.

Leadership Summit: Envisioning and equipping Christians with leadership gifts and responsibilities; broadcast live via satellite to eighteen cities across North America.

Contagious Evangelism Conference: Encouragement and training for churches and church leaders who want to be strategic in reaching lost people for Christ.

Small Groups Conference: Exploring how developing a church *of* small groups can play a vital role in developing authentic Christian community that leads to spiritual transformation.

PREVAILING CHURCH REGIONAL WORKSHOPS

Each year the WCA team leads several, two-day training events in select cities across the United States. Some twenty day-long workshops are offered in topic areas including leadership, next-generation ministries, small groups, arts and worship, evangelism, spiritual gifts, financial stewardship, and spiritual formation. These events make quality training more accessible and affordable to larger groups of staff and volunteers.

To find out more about Prevailing Church Regional Workshops, visit our website at www.willowcreek.com.

WILLOW CREEK RESOURCES™

Churches can look to Willow Creek Resources™ for a trusted channel of ministry tools in areas of leadership, evangelism, spiritual gifts, small groups, drama, contemporary music, financial stewardship, spiritual transformation, and more. For ordering information, call (800) 570-9812 or visit our website at www.willowcreek.com.

WCA MEMBERSHIP

Membership in the Willow Creek Association as well as attendance at WCA Conferences is for churches, ministries, and leaders who hold to a historic, orthodox understanding of biblical Christianity. The annual church membership fee of $249 provides substantial discounts for your entire team on all conferences and Willow Creek Resources, networking opportunities with other outreach-oriented churches, a bimonthly newsletter, a subscription to the *Defining Moments* monthly audio journal for leaders, and more.

Willow Creek Association
P.O. Box 3188, Barrington, IL 60011-3188
Phone: (800) 570-9812 or (847) 765-0070
Fax: (888) 922-0035 or (847) 765-5046
Web: www.willowcreek.com